A Student's Guide to AFRICAN AMERICAN Genealogy

Oryx American Family Tree Series

A Student's Guide to AFRICAN AMERICAN Genealogy

By Anne E. Johnson
and Adam Merton Cooper

Oryx Press
1996

Library of Congress Cataloging-in-Publication Data
Johnson, Anne E.
    A student's guide to African American genealogy / by Anne E.
Johnson and Adam Merton Cooper.
        p.   cm. — (The Oryx American family tree)
    Includes bibliographical references and index.
    ISBN 0-89774-972-3
    1. Afro-Americans—Genealogy—Handbooks, manuals, etc.
2. Afro-Americans—History—Bibliography.   3. Afro-Americans—
Genealogy—Bibliography.   I. Cooper, Adam Merton.   II. Title.
III. Series: Oryx American family tree.
E185.96.J57   1996
929'.1'08996073—dc20   95-41357
                                                           CIP

Contents

Chapter 1. A Heritage to Celebrate, 1
Back to Africa, 4
Be Proud and Realistic, 6
Resources, 9
  Starting Your Exploration, 9
  African American Language and Culture, 11
  African Language and Culture, 21

Chapter 2. Immigration in Chains, 25
The Modern Slave Trade, 25
Slave Life, 30
The End of the Slave Trade, 35
Resources, 38
  Africa: Past and Present, 38
  The Slave Trade, 44
  Slavery and Slave Life, 46

Chapter 3. Freedom and the African Cultural Diaspora, 49
The African Cultural Diaspora, 58
Resources, 61
  Free Blacks and Freedmen, 61
  Reconstruction and Modern History, 62
  Success Stories, 65
  Modern Immigration, 71
  Video, 73
  African American Theater, Film and Television, 74
  African Films, 76
  African American Films, 78
  African Music, 80
  African American Music, 81
  African Dance, 86
  African American Dance, 88

Chapter 4. Getting Started on Your Search, 91
Talking to Your Relatives, 91
Organizing Your Search, 93

Graveyards, 98
Working in the Library, 99
Resources, 102
  Searching in the United States: Manuals, Bibliographies, 102
  Societies and Journals, 106
  Attics and Heirlooms, 108
  Graveyards, 110
  Oral Tradition, 112

Chapter 5. The Census, and What It Doesn't Tell, 116
Interracial Unions, 122
Resources, 126

Chapter 6. Searching for Slaves, 131
County Deed Books, 132
Colored Troops, 133
Early Black Organizations, 134
Working Back Toward the Middle Passage, 137
Resources, 140
  General References and Indexes, 140
  Libraries, 142

Chapter 7. High-Tech Genealogy, 144
Resources, 147
  Family History on Computer, 147
  The Internet, 148

Chapter 8. Nontraditional Families and Family Issues, 149
Resources, 152
  Registers/Support Groups/Advocacy for Adoptees, 152
  Adoption and Other Family Issues, 153

Chapter 9. Preserving Your Family History, 156
Family Tree, 156
Oral History, 157
Written History, 158
Resources, 161
  Writing Your Family History, 161
  Great Writing by African Americans, 162

Glossary, 166
Index, 168

Chapter 1
A Heritage to Celebrate

Today in the United States a young person of any race is likely to blast a Janet Jackson tape while driving a date to the latest Denzel Washington movie. At home in front of the television you can cheer as Michael Jordan makes another slam dunk, or listen to what General Colin Powell has to say about the latest national security issues.

Today there are African American heroes. There are black men and women in every walk of life whom young people can look up to. Some of them are movie and sports stars or awe-inspiring leaders like Dr. Martin Luther King, Jr. Some are hard-working professionals or homemakers who never get much recognition. All of these people have made a great contribution to American society.

It has not been an easy road for African Americans to be recognized as citizens in this country, let alone as celebrities and leaders. Ever since the era of slavery, whenever racism has reared its head, black Americans have looked to their African roots to give them a sense of solidarity and self-worth. Although slaves were torn from their homeland and separated from their families and societies, their spiritual strength could not be taken from them. Their relationship with natural and supernatural forces was imbedded in their worldview from hundreds of years of cultural development. The spirits of their ancestors were no less venerated because their bodies were buried on another continent. In fact, those spirits gained more power because they brought a unity to a dispersed and disenfranchised population.

Most slaves came to the Caribbean or the United States from West Africa. In their home societies, there were men or women who were considered leaders. In most traditional

Dr. Martin Luther King, Jr., and other civil rights leaders encouraged African Americans to be proud of their heritage.

African societies the spheres of human life and the gods that make life possible were not (and are not) separated. Therefore, political chiefs were often priests as well, and shamans served as political advisers. People who became leaders in slave society had often been trained in the mystic arts of African religion and also possessed gifts of political persuasion. Slaves looked to these leaders to guide their actions and to give them spiritual comfort. This combination of religious and political leadership in one person has continued to inspire the African American community as they struggle against racism. Dr. Martin Luther King, Jr., and Malcolm X are outstanding examples.

African Americans have made great strides toward overcoming racism by working together. Slaves' religious meetings were places where a slave could feel like a person as well as a part of a community. Such meetings sometimes gave birth to slave revolts. In 1955, after Rosa Parks was arrested for refusing to give up her bus seat to a white passenger, leaders in the black community of Montgomery, Alabama, worked round the clock to organize a protest. The result was a complete boycott of the bus system by every African American in Montgomery, even those who depended on public transportation to get to work.

This kind of grass-roots unity was essential and effective throughout the civil rights movement. Political activists succeeded in getting many affirmative action laws passed, culminating in the Civil Rights Act of 1964, which made racial discrimination a violation of federal law. Yet no number of laws could change the opinion of racists who refused to see blacks as equal to themselves. Some of those racists were in high places. They were school chancellors, mayors, and governors. They simply refused to comply with the laws. But despite their resistance, the laws and attitudes of the country changed. It was through the grass-roots movements—boycotts, sit-ins, riots, marches—that thousands of ordinary citizens, black and white, expressed their outrage at discrimination.

The new sense of empowerment brought by the civil

rights movement inspired black Americans to celebrate their African roots. Genealogy proved to be a very personal way to pay respect to the African ancestors whose lives were spent in slavery. Until the 1960s it had been close to impossible for blacks to trace their family histories, except through oral traditions preserved by the family itself. Segregation laws from the late nineteenth century allowed African Americans to be barred from the research facilities that held essential genealogical documents. When these facilities were finally opened to people of all ethnicities, many blacks tried to satisfy their curiosity about their ancestors.

Back to Africa

The most spectacular example of black genealogy from the 1970s is Alex Haley's *Roots*. The story told by Haley was the story of millions of African Americans. He showed how his ancestors had been stolen from their native home, shipped across the Atlantic like cargo, sold like livestock, and forced to live in servitude and squalor as slaves on a plantation. The book was a best-seller, and the television series made from it had the largest viewing audience of all time.

Nonblacks read or saw *Roots* and felt horror and shame. Most of them had never imagined the realities of slavery. Some also felt great admiration for how far African Americans had come in leaving that terrible past behind. Blacks recognized their own roots in Haley's story. They saw how empowering it is to trace your family tree. They, too, wanted to understand what their slave ancestors suffered and what they were forced to leave behind.

Alex Haley was fortunate in his search. For one thing, he was a gifted writer who was able to combine documented fact seamlessly with believable fiction. Also, during the research process his luck was uncanny: His ancestors had held on to their African surname when they came to America. This practically never happened. He managed to find living relatives who could remember essential information. He found the slave trader and ship that were responsible for transporting the first of his ancestors to be taken

LeVar Burton starred in the stunning and, to many people, shocking television production of Alex Haley's *Roots* in 1977.

from Africa. Haley had the time and money to visit Africa and do research in national libraries there and to speak to village elders through interpreters.

All blacks in the United States have roots in Africa, even if their ancestors lived in the Caribbean or South America for centuries before coming to this country. In the vast majority of cases, those roots have been obliterated. There is no way for most African Americans to know exactly where in Africa their ancestors lived before they were sold as slaves.

Europeans buying slaves in West Africa to sell in the American colonies generally did not know themselves exactly where their victims came from. The slaves were prisoners of more powerful African groups, who had raided villages and brought the survivors to the west coast to sell. Once in the possession of the Europeans, people of different African ethnic groups were mixed together and families were split up. The British merchants feared that if the slaves could communicate with one another they might incite revolt.

Perhaps an ancestor passed on an African name; perhaps the new slaves kept an oral tradition alive that preserved details about their lives in Africa; perhaps ship records survive that describe a slave with a ritual tattoo or scar that only your ancestor had and that links him or her with a certain people in Africa. . . . These are the kinds of situations that you must hope for if you want to find specific roots in Africa. Once such links are suggested on this side of the Atlantic, it is necessary to travel to Africa, seeking some elder who can remember your ancestor's family through oral history.

Be Proud and Realistic

This book concentrates on how to trace your roots back to your ancestors' arrival in America. Most people, including professional genealogists, find this a big enough challenge. Unlike people of European background, African Americans cannot usually rely on government and legal documents for information about the centuries before the Civil War. Slaves were seldom able to read or write, and they had no legal

This lithograph depicts a slaver branding a slave with a red-hot firebrand before he is shipped from the African coast.

rights as citizens. A person of British American descent can hope to find some of her ancestors' wills and other records back to the seventeenth century. The descendant of a slave will be lucky to learn in which state his ancestor lived in 1850.

When they came to this country as slaves, Africans were cut off from their cultures, their languages, and their loved ones. Nothing could obliterate the memories of these things while the African-born ancestors were still alive. Early African Americans did their best to preserve both their past and their present through oral history. Since the abolition of slavery and the granting of long-deserved civil rights to African Americans, much of this oral history has been lost. You can make a huge contribution by unburying and saving any part of that past that you can. You don't have to find your exact roots in Africa to accomplish something very important. Genealogy depends on the ability to move backward in time from one generation to the previous one. A lot of generations may have been lost between you and your first ancestor to come to America from Africa. If you can restore some of those lost ancestors, some of that lost history and heritage, you will have done important work indeed.

Even if you are not African American yourself, you may be intrigued by the fascinating and challenging aspects of African American family history research. You may simply want to read about the process, or you may wish to trace the background of a friend or a historical figure. This book will illustrate for you the unique and important contributions of African Americans to American culture.

By all means, if you are African American, try to trace your roots back to Africa. You may be one of the lucky ones who get the thrill of a lifetime finding evidence of their own past among one of Africa's indigenous cultures. Certainly, go to Africa if you ever get a chance, whether or not you intend to do serious genealogical research. After all, if you are an African American, then Africa is the first home of your ancestors. You are connected to that land by blood.

Resources

STARTING YOUR EXPLORATION

Chocolate, Deborah Newton. *Kwanzaa*. Chicago: Children's Press, 1990.

The festival of Kwanzaa was developed in the United States in 1966 as a way for African Americans to remember, celebrate, and reinforce their African heritage at holiday time. This vibrant book shows the basics of the holiday. Learn about Kwanzaa, then teach your kid sister!

David, Jay, ed. *Growing Up Black: From Slave Days to the Present*, rev. ed. New York: Avon, 1992.

This book will introduce you to some of the best-known African American writers. Their autobiographical accounts may be especially interesting to you if you are planning to write your own autobiography.

Halliburton, Warren J. *Africa Today*. Columbus, OH: Silver Burdett, 1992–93.

An eight-volume series with volumes on topics such as African wildlife, African celebrations, and Saharan nomads.

***The Heritage Library of African Peoples*. New York: Rosen Publishing Group, 1995–96.**

A fifty-six-volume series on the peoples of east, west, central, and southern Africa. Each book provides a historical perspective on a people and describes their customs and beliefs. Already-published titles include *Maasai, Pokot, Kipsigis, Agikuyu, Rendille,* and *Gabra.* Full-color photos and maps illustrate the text.

Hull, Robert. *African Stories*. **New York: Thomson Learning, 1993.**

Get a taste for the rich oral tradition in Africa with this collection of classic African tales.

Johnson, Angela. *Toning the Sweep*. **New York: Orchard Books, 1993.**

On a visit to her grandmother Ola, who is dying of cancer in her house in the desert, fourteen-year-old Emmie hears many stories about the past and comes to a better understanding of relatives both dead and living.

Lotu, Denise. *Father and Son*. **New York: Philomel Books, 1992.**

This illustrated poetry-story for young people celebrates the relationship between an African American father and his son in the low country of South Carolina. They get to know one another as they spend time together and teach each other how to do things.

Ofosu-Appiah, L. H. *People in Bondage: African Slavery Since the 15th Century*. **Minneapolis: Runestone Press, 1993.**

This is probably the best short history of the slave trade written for young people. Starting from its most ancient history, slavery is traced to its point of concentration in the West Indies and America, comparing and contrasting situations in different periods and under different laws, through the U.S. Civil War.

Pinkney, Andrea Davis. *Seven Candles for Kwanzaa*. **New York: Dial Books for Young Readers, 1993.**

Suppose your kid brother asks you about Kwanzaa. What would you tell him? Prepare yourself by reading the basics about the holiday in Pinkney's book. Candlelighting is but one part of the festival developed in the United States in 1966 to encourage African Americans to embrace and celebrate their African heritage.

Pinkney, J. Brian. *Max Found Two Sticks.* **New York: Simon & Schuster, 1994.**

This is a story for young readers about the freedom and power you can find in music. Although he doesn't feel like talking, a young African American boy finds his voice by drumming on various objects—bucket, hat boxes, garbage cans—echoing the city sounds around him.

Reef, Catherine. *Black Fighting Men: A Proud History.* **New York: Twenty-First Century Books, 1994.**

African American soldiers have fought in all of the major conflicts in which the United States has been involved. They have waged a double battle against foreign enemies and racism. This book profiles several African American soldiers.

Stepto, Michele, ed. *Our Song, Our Toil: The Story of American Slavery as Told by Slaves.* **Brookfield, CT: Millbrook Press, 1994.**

Excerpts from letters, diaries, and autiobiographies of slaves tell their stories in their own words. The vivid narratives are illustrated by photographs.

Sullivan, Charles, ed. *Children of Promise: African-American Literature and Art for Young People.* **New York: Abrams, 1991.**

A well-illustrated anthology of the work of African Americans from the time of slavery to the present.

Turner, Glennette. *Running for Our Lives.* **New York: Holiday House, 1994.**

An eleven-year-old tells the story of his family and their escape from a Missouri plantation via the Underground Railroad.

AFRICAN AMERICAN LANGUAGE AND CULTURE

Abrahams, Roger D. *Singing the Master: The Emergence of African American Culture in the Plantation South.* **New York: Pantheon, 1992.**

African ideas have affected every aspect of culture in the United States, including dance, music, literature, humor, and religious worship. There is no way to overstate these contributions to aspects of life that we take for granted today. This book describes the development of a distinct African American culture.

Alexander, Lois K. *Blacks in the History of Fashion.* New York: Harlem Institute of Fashion, 1982.

Blacks have influenced fashion in many ways. This book deals with professional designers who show their works on the runways of New York and Paris, theater designers who were influenced by the long dresses of the French Caribbean, as well as stars such as Michael Jackson whose trademark clothing has been emulated by millions as a fad.

Almeida, Bira. *Capoeira: A Brazilian Art Form.* Palo Alto, CA: Sun Wave, 1981.

Capoeira is a martial art developed by the Brazilian descendants of the Yoruba of West Africa. Learn about the African origins and Brazilian evolution of this graceful, mesmerizing, dancelike self-defense technique in Almeida's fascinating book.

***Baking in the Sun: Visionary Images from the South.* Lafayette: University of Southwest Louisiana, 1987.**

The collection of Sylvia and Warren Lowe is photographed with accompanying text. These are fascinating pieces from the last century of slavery in the United States. The sculptures and paintings seem to reveal secrets from the agonized hearts of their makers, but at the same time betray a life-strengthening sense of humor and joy of existence.

***The Beat.* Los Angeles: Bongo Productions.**

This periodical is your best source for up-to-the-minute reviews of African and diaspora music. It includes reggae,

Caribbean, World Music, and every combination that has ever been recorded. Available bimonthly (twelve dollars for a year) from Bongo Prod., P.O. Box 65856, Los Angeles, CA 90065.

The Black Americana Collector. Bimonthly. Baltimore, MD: R. Brooks.

Black Ethnic Collectibles. Quarterly. Hyattsville, MD: Ethnic Treasures.

These two journals are dedicated to African American folk art. They feature photographs of and articles about pieces from many periods and places in American history, from the woodcarving of Southern slaves to urban acrylic painting from modern-day Chicago. Also included are documents and personal belongings reminiscent of the struggle for freedom by both the slaves and the civil rights movement in the 1960s.

Crahan, Margaret, and Knight, Franklin W. *Africa and the Caribbean: The Legacies of a Link*. Baltimore: Johns Hopkins University Press, 1979.

African slaves were being shipped to the Caribbean to grow sugar even before they were shipped to the American colonies. This book celebrates the music, dance, religious ceremonies, language, dress, and other cultural developments that grew from those early years of contact between Africans and Europeans in the West Indies.

Feather, Leonard. *Encyclopedia of Jazz in the '60s and '70s*. New York: Horizon Press, 1969.

Feather was one of the most famous writers on jazz music. This encyclopedia, in volumes covering a decade each, is a great resource written while it was all happening. It features alphabetical entries by artist, complete discographies (up to publication date), and lots of photos.

Ferris, William. *Afro-American Art and Crafts*. Boston, MA: G. K. Hall, 1983.

Ferris's book covers textiles, sculpture, painting, and other traditional black American crafts from Florida to Oregon. It also provides a history of folk-art trade among African Americans. Some people set up co-ops to produce and sell their handiwork after the Reconstruction period.

Freeman, Roland. *Southern Roads/City Pavements: Photographs of Black Americans.* **New York: International Center of Photography, 1981.**

From the farms of Mississippi to the boardrooms of Chicago and the House of Representatives in Washington: Leaf through more than 100 pages of photos of African Americans and where they live and work in the United States, taken by a contemporary African American photographer.

Galembo, Phyllis. *Divine Inspiration: From Benin to Bahia.* **Albuquerque: University of New Mexico Press, 1993.**

A collection of writings by scholars of the African diaspora, illustrated with stunning photographs. Contributors include Robert Farris Thompson, writing on "Art and Altars of the Black Atlantic World."

Geraty, Virginia Mixson. *Bittle en' t'ing: Gullah Cooking with Maum Chrish'.* **Orangeburg, SC: Sandlapper Publishing, 1992.**

Maum Chrish' rustles up Southern soul food with a distinct African flavor in South Carolina. Look over these seventy-eight pages of down-home recipes and luscious illustrations, and let your mouth water!

Gray, John. *Ashé: Traditional Religion and Healing in Subsaharan Africa and the Diaspora.* **Westport, CT: Greenwood Press, 1989.**

This is an international bibliography, arranged by subject. Beliefs, worship practices, herbal remedies, voodoo, curses, and oaths are among the aspects of traditional religion covered.

Guffy, Ossie, and Ledner, Caryl. *Ossie: The Autobiography of a Black Woman.* **New York: W. W. Norton & Co., 1971.**

Not quite as famous as Malcolm X, Ossie Guffy has still seen fit to tell her story. Read about one member of an African American community trying to prosper and retain dignity in the United States through turbulent times.

Hareven, Tamara K., ed. *Anonymous Americans: Explorations in Nineteenth-Century Social History.* **Englewood Cliffs, NJ: Prentice-Hall, 1971.**

Although most black slaves were not literate, neither were they silent. L. W. Levine tries to get a glimpse into the mind of the slave through his songs. His essay in this collection, "Slave Songs and Slave Consciousness: An Exploration in Neglected Sources," suggests what he found. "Free at Last" by L. F. Litwack is also of interest.

Home and Yard: Black Folk Life Expressions in L.A. **Los Angeles: California Afro-American Museum, 1987.**

Folk art is not something made only on farms and in log cabins. Urban folk art has become an increasingly fascinating genre throughout the twentieth century. These are photos of recent pieces, very personal comments on race relations, poverty, power, and other essential issues.

Hughes, Langston, and Meltzer, Milton. *Black Magic: A Pictorial History of the African American in the Performing Arts.* **New York: Da Capo Press, 1990; reprint of 1967 publication, with new foreword.**

The famous poet Langston Hughes put together this book as a way of showing respect and appreciation for the hundreds of actors, singers, dancers, and musicians who helped to put African Americans in the spotlight. Many of these people were underappreciated while they were working because of their race, and Hughes's book helps to rectify that for the future.

Johnson, Howard, and Pines, Jim. *Reggae: Deep Roots Music*. New York: Proteus Books, 1982.

Read about the first twenty years of the music Jamaica brought to the world. The religion of Ras Tafari (now Rastafarianism), the quest for social justice, and the careers of musicians like Bob Marley and Jimmy Cliff are some of the points covered in the book.

Joyce, Donald Franklin, ed. *Blacks in the Humanities, 1750–1984*. Westport, CT: Greenwood Press, 1984.

African Americans have made contributions in the arts and scholarship for centuries. This bibliography is a guide to these writers, teachers, visual artists, and performing artists.

Kitwana, Bakari. *The Rap on Gangsta Rap: Who Run It?: Gangsta Rap and Visions of Black Violence*. Chicago: Third World Press, 1994.

This excellent overview of hip-hop and its place in African American and the wider American culture includes sections on "Rap in the black muscial tradition," "The politics of rap lyrics," "Community need, commercial desire," and "A victim's worldview: gangstas, players, pimps, hustlers."

Kofsky, Frank. *Black Nationalism and the Revolution in Music*. New York: Pathfinder, 1970.

The author claims that the development of bebop and modern jazz were the black musical community's reaction to and comment upon urban racism in the 1940s, '50s, and '60s. He concentrates on the John Coltrane Quartet for interviews and musical examples.

Krehbiel, Henry Edward. *Afro-American Folksongs: A Study in Racial and National Music*. New York: F. Ungar, 1962.

Influenced by the rhythms of Africa, the sorrow and pain of slave existence, and the ecstasy of religious worship, black American folksong is a rich source for understanding the life of the people. This book considers how the music reflects the singers' identity and opinions.

Livingston, Jane, and Beardsley, John. *Black Folk Art in America, 1930–1980*. Jackson: University Press of Mississippi, 1982.

This is an especially interesting book because of the period it covers. The mid-twentieth century was an era of struggle and self-discovery for the African American community. But even as folk art began to reflect current events and political opinion, the vibrant shapes of life from ancient African traditions still informed these works.

Lomax, Alan. *The Land Where the Blues Began*. New York: Pantheon, 1993.

An exploration of the origins of the blues. Lomax defied threats of imprisonment and violence when he began his work in the deep South during the days of segregation.

Long, Richard A. *Africa and America: Essays in Afro-American Culture*. Atlanta: Center for African and African-American Studies, Atlanta University, 1981.

Long's excellent essays make wonderful food for thought—and action. Learn about the famous scholar W. E. B. Du Bois, the folklore of Africa and the African diaspora, and how the Harlem Renaissance helped black Americans awaken to their African origins and heritage.

McClester, Cedric. *Kwanzaa: Everything You Always Wanted to Know but Didn't Know Where to Ask*. New York: Gumbs & Thomas, 1985.

Concise yet comprehensive, this thirty-six-page work sets out all the basics of the American festival that began in 1966. The various rituals are succinctly described, and their connections to traditional African practices are explained.

Mitchell, Patricia B. *Soul on Rice: African Influences on American Cooking*. Chatham, VA: Patricia B. Mitchell, 1993.

A collection of anecdotes and recipes about African culinary contributions.

Moe, John F. *Amazing Grace: The Life and Work of Elijah Pierce*. Columbus, OH: Martin Luther King, Jr. Center for Performing and Cultural Arts, 1990.

Elijah Pierce was an African American artist from Ohio. His woodcarvings, full of the life of the artist's heritage and humor, have been delighting people for a century. This book is a companion to a museum exhibit and includes photographs of the works as well as commentary.

Robertson, Linda. *The Complete Kwanzaa Celebration Book*. Detroit: Creative Acrylic Concepts, 1994.

If you're going to celebrate Kwanzaa, this book tells you what you need to know. What meals are traditionally eaten? What about the candlelighting ceremonies? These and other such questions are answered clearly and thoroughly.

Rogers, J. A. *Nature Knows No Colorline*. New York: Holga M. Rogers, 1952.

There is evidence, from a large number of coats of arms depicting blacks, that descendants of Africa have lived in Europe for a thousand years. This book discusses those Africans who settled or roamed in Britain, Germany, and Switzerland.

Rosen, Roger, and Sevastiades, Patra McSharry, eds. *Celebration: Visions and Voices of the African Diaspora*. New York: Rosen Publishing Group, 1994.

A collection of writings on such varied topics as capoeira, an African-derived martial art, and "playing the dozens," a form of verbal jousting. Also includes several fiction pieces and an essay by the scholar Cornel West.

Southern, Eileen, ed. *The Music of Black Americans: A History*. New York: W. W. Norton & Co., 1983.

This history of African American music covers the period from 1619 to 1980. It includes slave songs, gospel, blues, and jazz, as well as African Americans on the concert stages of Europe and the United States in the nineteenth and twentieth centuries.

————. *Readings in Black American Music.* **New York: W. W. Norton & Co., 1983.**

This fine compilation offers excerpts from articles, books, and essays about African American music. Sources include *Movin' on Up* by Mahalia Jackson, Dizzy Gillespie's *To Be or Not to Bop*, *My Bondage and My Freedom* by Frederick Douglass, and Richard Allen's *A Collection of Hymns and Spiritual Songs*. It is intended as a companion piece to *The Music of Black Americans: A History*, above.

Stearns, Marshall W. *The Story of Jazz.* **New York: Oxford University Press, 1956.**

The fascinating story of the first decades of jazz. The journey begins in Africa, moves through the Caribbean to slave communities in the South, takes in some influences from Euro-American music, and goes urban. The rest is history and great music.

Stewart, Gary. *Breakout: Profiles in African Rhythm.* **Chicago: University of Chicago Press, 1992.**

These are short biographies of many pop musicians in Africa, including Docteur Nico, Orlando Julius Ekemode, and Fela Anikulapo-Kuti. The profiles cover their subjects' role models, political stance (when it affects their music), opinions about the future of African music, and discography.

Stuckey, Sterling. *Going Through the Storm: The Influence of African American Art in History.* **New York: Oxford University Press, 1994.**

This study considers every aspect of African-based American culture and how it has shaped developments in the arts all over the world. Includes discussions of folklore, philosophy, dance, song, music, and even nationalism.

Thompson, Robert Farris. *Flash of the Spirit.* New York: Vintage, 1983.

The author shows how five African civilizations have informed and are reflected in the different facets of African American culture in the United States.

Tudor, Dean, and Tudor, Nancy. *Black Music.* Littleton, CO: Libraries Unlimited, 1979.

The Tudors offer a partial discography that includes gospel, blues, soul, R & B, and reggae.

Turner, Lorenzo Dow. *Africanisms in the Gullah Dialect.* New York: Arno Press, 1969.

The Gullah people of Georgia and South Carolina speak a dialect of English that is full of words and phrases derived from West African languages. Even their nicknames can be shown to have African origins. Turner explains how it all came about.

Vlach, John Michael. *By the Work of their Hands: Studies in Afro-American Folklife.* Charlottesville: University Press of Virginia, 1991.

The author examines the African American tradition in folk art and architecture and highlights the stories of several artisans.

Weekley, Carolyn J. *Joshua Johnson: Freeman and Early American Portrait Painter.* Williamsburg: Abbey Aldrich Rockefeller Folk Art Center, Maryland Historical Society, 1987.

Joshua Johnson was one of the lucky freedmen who had such talent that he was able to make a living at his craft. Defying the odds in pre-Civil War Baltimore, Johnson painted high-quality oil portraits of politicians and ladies of society.

Wiley, Ralph. *Why Black People Tend to Shout: Cold Facts and Wry Views from a Black Man's World.* **Secaucus, NJ: Carol Publishing Group, 1991.**

A humorous, sometimes biting work about African American cultural characteristics, written from the inside.

Williams, Joseph J. *Psychic Phenomena of Jamaica.* **New York: The Dial Press, 1934.**

Williams introduces the reader to belief in the supernatural in Jamaica. Topics include Asante cultural influence in Jamaica, witchcraft, magic, ghosts and poltergeists, and funeral customs.

Wilson, James L. *Clementine Hunter, American Folk Artist.* **Gretna, LA: Pelican, 1988.**

Clementine Hunter was an African American painter in Louisiana in the mid-twentieth century. Her work was influenced by the long-lived traditions of Africa as well as by vibrant splashes of the Cajun world around her.

Wolfram, Walter A., and Clarke, Nona H., eds. *Black-White Speech Relationships.* **Washington, DC: Center for Applied Linguistics, 1971.**

The Africans who were shipped to America acquired a new language from the whites already living there. But blacks have made contributions to the way English is spoken. Similarities and differences between the speech patterns of blacks and whites are discussed and explained.

AFRICAN LANGUAGE AND CULTURE

Blier, Suzanne Preston. *African Vodun: Art, Psychology and Power.* **Chicago: University of Chicago Press, 1995.**

In over 450 pages, the author tells the reader about this fascinating belief system as it thrives today in Benin and Togo. Blier shows that much can be learned about vodun (voodoo) by looking at the sculptures and idols that its adherents create. A useful collection of maps, photos, and illustrations complete the presentation.

Gibrill, Martin. *African Food and Drink*. East Sussex, U.K.: Wayland, 1989.

This book gives you a start on learning about the eating and drinking habits of modern Africans.

Hafner, Dorinda. *A Taste of Africa*. Berkeley, CA: Ten Speed Press, 1993.

This cookbook includes over 100 traditional African recipes. Some of the cooking processes and ingredients are altered so that you can prepare the dishes at home. Why not bring a taste of Africa into your own kitchen?

Haskins, James, and Biondi, Joann. *From Afar to Zulu: A Dictionary of African Cultures*. New York: Walker, 1995.

This is the place to find the basic facts on just about any African ethnic group. Find out how long the Shona have lived in their current territory, whether the Shilluk can understand the language of the Nuer, how many Edo there are today, and more. Illustrations and maps help make this reference easy and fun to use.

Johnson, Adrienne M. "Our Road to African Womanhood in Ghana." *YSB*, March 1995, pp. 27–28.

Johnson, an African American teenager, describes her visit to Ghana with her mother and their participation in traditional Ghanaian women's ceremonies.

Konrad, Zinta. *Ewe Comic Heroes: Trickster Tales in Togo*. New York: Garland Publishing, 1994.

Trickster tales are common in West Africa. They feature a character, usually an animal, who uses cunning to achieve a goal—even if that goal is simply mischief! This book has tales from the Ewe people of Togo, along with commentary.

Little, Kenneth Lindsay. *The Mende of Sierra Leone: A West African People in Transition.* New York: Humanities Press, 1967.

Look on as the Mende contribute to the progress of Sierra Leone while retaining their identity and traditions. This book also allows readers a glimpse into Mende secret societies.

Locke, David. *Drum Damba: Talking Drum Lessons.* Crown Point, IN: White Cliffs Media Co., 1990.

This text by a diligent collector of Ghanaian folk traditions offers beginning instructions in *damba*, the drum-based dance music of the Dagomba, a people of northern Ghana. The book includes helpful illustrations, and the technique of drum master Abubakari Lunna is used in examples.

Lystad, Robert Arthur. *The Ashanti: A Proud People.* New Brunswick, NJ: Rutgers University Press, 1958.

The Asante (Ashanti) of central Ghana built a large and powerful empire in the eighteenth and nineteenth centuries. Their power was broken by the British only after decades of fierce fighting. Read about their customs and history in Lystad's memorable book.

Ojibo, A. Okion, ed. *Young and Black in Africa.* New York: Random House, 1971.

This broad collection of stories by African authors documents what it's like to grow up in Africa. It includes "Seized into Slavery" by O. Equiano, "My Sister Is Born" by F. Selormey, "Grandfather and Granddaughter" by C. Wacjuma, "I Am Hit by a Night Stick" by R. Gatheru, and "An African's Adventures in America" by B. Fafunwa.

Wright, Rose Helen. *Fun and Festival from Africa.*
New York: Friendship Press, 1967.

A select group of African festivals form the subject of this colorfully illustrated book. Learn about the cuisine, dance, and songs that have been part of African celebrations for centuries.

Chapter 2
Immigration in Chains

Between about AD 1000 and 1500, great empires were flourishing in the grasslands of West Africa, around the Niger River. People had lived in the area for tens of thousands of years. By this time they had so mastered their environment that they were able to develop complex societies of astounding wealth and advancement. A vigorous trade was maintained both with the Arabs to their north and the forest and coastal peoples to their south and west. When these empires declined, large numbers of inhabitants saw fit to move away toward the coast, taking with them aspects of their culture. Other parts of West Africa were developing kingdoms and city-states of their own at this time.

Slavery was a feature of many African societies. For thousands of years slavery had been practiced in nearly all of the powerful kingdoms of the ancient world. The great kingdoms of Africa were no exception. For these groups, slavery was not a moral issue but a question of economics. Any empire's strength grew only until it had conquered more land than it could afford to exploit. This could mean farming, mining, building, or hunting on land gained through military conquest. Once it had passed the point of being able to exploit the land, the empire sought to maintain its power by enslaving those prisoners taken during the conquest and forcing them to work the land.

The Modern Slave Trade
When Europeans arrived in Africa in the fifteenth century they were at first more interested in buying gold, ivory, and other such goods from the Africans than they were in buying slaves. As the years went on, however, and the European

It is difficult to trace one's ancestry in Africa because slaves were brought from many parts of the continent before they were shipped overseas. Slave traders treated slaves as little better than animals, cutting them off from their cultures and families.

colonies in the Americas grew, more and more slaves were purchased to work the plantations. Slaves became the most important commodity traded.

The "modern" slave trade—the trade in human beings between powerful Africans and Europeans—began with the Portuguese in 1480. Some of the Africans bought then were sent to Europe, but most were shipped to the new Portuguese colonies in South America. In 1538, Africans were first brought to Brazil by Portugese slavers. By then, the Portugese slave trade followed a triangular pattern. In Portugal, European goods were loaded on the ships, which sailed to African ports. There the merchandise was traded for slaves, who were then loaded on the ships and sold in Brazil for gold. The ships then returned to Portugal for more merchandise. Over the next 150 years the slave trade was joined by England, France, Spain, and Holland.

The European presence changed the face of slavery in Africa. Powerful Africans on the Guinea Coast of West Africa set up an elaborate business system from which both they and the Europeans profited. Europeans were allowed to build forts in the coastal territories of West Africa. These forts, for which Europeans also paid rent to the African hosts, served partly as temporary stock houses where slaves were held until their slave ship sailed.

The acquisition of slaves became a blatantly cruel process. Europeans were rarely allowed to seize their own slaves. They had to buy them—for guns, cannons, rum, and other European goods—from West African middlemen. The Africans procured slaves by attacking weaker groups inland and selling the captives. The frightened victims of these raids were tied into coffles, trains of prisoners bound by the neck onto long poles. They were force-marched through the wilderness to the west coast. Those who became ill were beaten and left for dead.

This was only the beginning of their agony. Those who survived the march in coffle were sold to European agents. They were herded into a section of the fort and crowded into a large room with little light and no place to sleep or

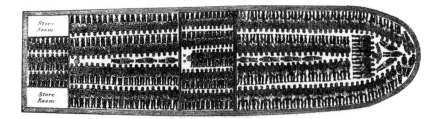

This lithograph of the lower deck of a slave ship shows the horribly cramped conditions in which many slaves traveled to the Americas. Many people did not survive the voyage.

relieve oneself, save the floor. There they remained, with little food or water, until a slave ship arrived to carry them off. Then they were packed onto a ship.

If they were "lucky," they were chained together on the deck. Otherwise they were stuffed below deck into a 5-foot-high hold with a platform dividing it into two $2\frac{1}{2}$-foot-high compartments. Besides disease and exhaustion, one of the most common causes of death on a slave ship was suffocation in the packed, unventilated hold. People who died of infectious disease were dumped overboard to prevent its spreading to more of the profitable cargo. Some captives were so terrified at these experiences that they committed— or attempted—suicide by jumping overboard or smashing their heads against the rails.

One of the tragic ironies of the modern slave trade is how the captives who survived the transatlantic crossing, or Middle Passage, were forced to contribute toward the furthering of slavery. On sugar plantations in the West Indies and South America, under ruthless working conditions, African slaves harvested and processed the sugarcane crop into molasses. The product was sent to distilleries on the northeast coast of America, where it was used to make rum. That rum, in turn, became the main item traded by Europeans to buy more slaves from Africa.

The first British ship to take slaves to North America arrived in 1619, when twenty captive Africans were brought to the settlement of Jamestown in Virginia. The Africa-to-

This lithograph of a slave auction in New York shows one typical manner in which slaves were traded upon arrival in America.

North America slave route did not become big business until the following century. During the 1600s, the colonist settlers exploited two forms of cheap labor. The first were Native Americans. This arrangement was not sustainable, however. Enslaved, the indigenous peoples died by the thousands, their population decimated by exposure to European diseases to which they had no resistance.

The other main source of American labor in the seventeenth century were convicts and indentured servants from Britain. After a contracted number of years of labor, indentured servants were granted freedom plus a small amount of land to own and work or a shop in which to start a business. Even the first African slaves were considered indentured servants. That is how some blacks became landowners in America at a very early date.

By the eighteenth century indentured servitude was no longer considered economically viable. Colonial landowners decided that they could not turn a big enough profit. On the other hand, to force fellow white Christians to work for nothing at all was considered immoral. Black Africans, however, looked different, and their traditional belief systems were incomprehensible to Europeans. Most American colonists had no trouble justifying the exploitation of a captive African labor force.

Slave Life

As Africans were headed across the Atlantic to the Americas, they could not imagine what was in store for them. When a slave ship docked in an American port, a crowd of prospective buyers assembled for the sale. These white people looked and behaved like nothing the Africans had ever seen. Part of the sale was called the "scramble." A market price was agreed upon by the seller and buyers. Then a gun was fired, and all the customers rushed on board, swarming among the slaves and trying to claim those few who still appeared fit and healthy. Of all they had endured up to now, little of the slaves' ordeal had been more horrifying than this spectacle of ogling, shouting white people.

Slaves were also sold by auction. Notices were printed,

describing the people for sale. If a slave seemed sickly, he or she would be thought worth very little. Some were sold for as little as one dollar. If a trader was very clever, he could make his captives appear healthier than they were, for instance, by rubbing oil on their skin. Many slave buyers were duped in this way, only to find that their purchase was ill or near death.

The community and family units of the African people were purposefully violated during the process of selling. Buyers feared that keeping intact a close-knit group like a family—or even unrelated people who spoke the same African language—would lead to rebellion. Mothers could do nothing but wail with grief as they and their children were sold to different masters.

Many of the buyers at slave ports were further middlemen, who took their purchases to their new homes on plantations, farms, or workshops. It was common to sell slaves directly to the Caribbean from Africa, and then to resell them to North America after a year or so. This was believed to help "acclimate" the slave to "civilized" culture. Slaves who had come by this circuitous route were considered to be worth more.

Although the Northern colonies kept very few slaves, the New England states were mostly responsible for slave traffic. Boston, Salem, and Newport grew wealthy as centers for rum merchants, seamen, and shipbuilders.

The real demand for slaves was in the South. Although today most people think of cotton as the primary plantation crop harvested by slaves, cotton was not important until the nineteenth century. During the colonial period, slaves cultivated and harvested three main products: tobacco, grown mainly in Virginia and Maryland, and indigo and rice in the Carolinas. The rice plantations were especially terrible places to work. The hot swamps necessary for growing this crop were so rife with malaria that the plantation owners usually chose to live far from their own estates. Their slaves, on the other hand, were forced to labor knee-deep in the filthy water from dawn to dusk.

Owners had a deep fear of slave rebellion. Colonies all

The slave rebellion led by Toussaint L'Ouverture in Haiti (then known as St. Domingue) realized the worst fears of slave owners, who had split up families and slaves speaking the same language in an effort to preclude revolt.

over the Americas instituted "slave codes." These laws of conduct on the part of slaves and owners were sometimes masked to appear to help the slaves. In reality, they were meant to keep the Africans in check.

Blacks were by no means docile during the period of slavery. Some ran away, some helped others to escape, some revolted, sometimes murdering their masters. Their owners tried to keep power from them. Codes were passed over the decades, reflecting the deepening fears of the slave-owning population. Here are some examples of the kinds of codes that were passed in various states.

- No slave may speak any language but English.
- No slave owner may teach his slaves to read and write, or allow them to be taught.
- A slave must have documented permission to be off his or her owner's land.
- A black person may not strike a white person in self-defense.
- Slaves may not play drums or blow horns.
- Slaves may not visit the houses of whites or free blacks.
- A group of slaves can meet only in the presence of a white.

In 1791 the owners' nightmare came true in Haiti, then called, by the French, St. Domingue. A self-educated black slave named Toussaint L'Ouverture led a huge, bloody rebellion on that island. The revolt sent a clear message throughout the slave-owning Americas.

That message could soon be heard much closer to home. Slave revolts in the United States were usually led, or at least inspired by, preachers. Religious leadership was the only position of power allowed to slaves. Slave communities encouraged preachers' authority. They needed the comfort and advice of a leader who understood their culture. The Christianity sermonized by these ministers was often mixed with aspects of traditional African animism and ancestor worship. The slave owners tried to take advantage of black preachers as liaisons between master and slave. Owners would hire religious leaders to tell their congregations that heaven opened its gates only to obedient slaves. Sometimes the preachers spoke as they were instructed. Just as often, though, they sowed the seeds of rebellion in the fertile imaginations of their flocks.

In 1800 two slave brothers named Gabriel and Martin, owned by Tom Prosser of Henrico County, Virginia, listened to such a sermon. It was about the courageous rebellion waged by the Israelites against their tormentors, the Egyptians. Armed with this paradigm from holy scripture, the two men worked tirelessly to organize the biggest slave revolt America had ever seen. The forces they mustered numbered in the thousands. Only the bizarre coincidence of sudden torrential rains kept the insurrection from succeeding. Despite what seemed like divine intervention, the area's slaveowners were thoroughly terrified.

The Methodist minister Denmark Vesey was a founder of the African Church of Charleston, North Carolina. He, too, was struck by the similarity between the plight of the ancient Israelites and that of African slaves. He told his congregation that to struggle for freedom would be pleasing to God. His arguments were all the more readily received because they were backed by Jack Pritchard ("Gullah Jack"), who was respected in the community for his knowledge of traditional African magic and medicine. Vesey and Pritchard led a slave revolt in 1822. They and many other participants were hanged for their courage.

The most famous American slave rebellion occurred in August 1831, in southeastern Virginia. This was not plantation country; slaves were used as servants and farmhands and were not treated as cruelly as were plantation slaves. The slave Nat Turner was even taught to read and write. The insurrection led by this preacher left sixty whites dead before Turner and others were caught and executed. Slave owners understood more clearly than ever the potential power of an African American community acting in solidarity.

The End of the Slave Trade

Throughout the late seventeenth and eighteenth centuries a growing number of white people were sincerely concerned about Africans as human beings. In the forefront of the earliest political opposition to slavery were the Quakers. The Quaker pamphleteer Anthony Benezet published two treatises about Guinea. Their contents, on the inhumanity of the slave trade, inspired many people in both the United States and England to become outspoken abolitionists. By the late eighteenth century a strong society for the abolition of slavery was working in France as well.

The first draft of the United States Declaration of Independence included a condemnation of slavery. The signers from Georgia and South Carolina, both major plantation states, were powerful enough to have the clause removed. The Southern states considered the use of slaves in their businesses as one of their rights as a political unit. The fear that government was becoming too centralized and that states were losing their right to govern themselves became an increasing problem among Southern states. Decades later, that discontent would explode into the Civil War.

In 1808—thanks to the human rights activism of abolitionists and the hope of the Southern states to avoid slave revolts—the U.S. government passed a law banning the importation of slaves. Such laws were passed at around the same time by European powers, affecting their colonies in South America and the Caribbean. Joint agreements were made among the world powers to police the ocean for illegal slaving vessels. Only Great Britain took its policing job seriously. The other countries turned a blind eye toward pirates, whose shipments of slaves helped keep their sugar plantations viable.

Two things must be understood about the abolition of the slave trade to the United States. First, it was not the same thing as the abolition of slavery. It meant only that new slaves could not be legally imported from Africa. There were plenty of slaves here already, and those had children and

EMANCIPATOR—EXTRA.

American Anti-Slavery Almanac for 1840.

The seven cuts following, are selected from thirteen, which may be found in the Anti-Slavery Almanac for 1840. They represent well-authenticated facts, and illustrate in various ways, the cruelties daily inflicted upon three millions of native born Americans, by their fellow-countrymen! A brief explanation follows each cut.

The peculiar " Domestic Institutions of our Southern brethren."

Selling a Mother from her Child.

Mothers with young Children at work in the field.

A Woman chained to a Girl, and a Man in irons at work in the field.

" They can't take care of themselves"; explained in an interesting article.

Hunting Slaves with dogs and guns. A Slave drowned by the dogs.

Servility of the Northern States in arresting and returning fugitive Slaves.

The movement for the abolition of slavery gained momentum throughout the eighteenth and nineteenth centuries. The *Emancipator* was an antislavery newspaper.

grandchildren who were also slaves. Besides, the illegal trade in slaves stepped in to fill the gap. Second, although the end of legal slave trading might look like a step toward the end of slavery itself, the law to stop trade was not passed on purely humanitarian grounds. The slave owners in the powerful Southern states allowed the law to be passed because they were terrified of a revolt like the one in Haiti sixteen years earlier. They had not changed their minds about the morality of keeping slaves.

By coincidence, the U.S. Southern states' demand for slaves grew intensely during the same decades that the law against the slave trade was being hammered out. A great change had come over the South, spurred on by a new machine. The cotton gin was invented in 1793, and for the first time cotton could be processed fast enough to be highly profitable to grow.

The amount of slave smuggling to the Deep South is evidenced by alarming statistics. The antislave importing law took effect in 1808. Yet some historians believe that between 1807 and 1840 the traffic of slaves to the United States doubled: In 1790 there were 700,000 slaves; by 1860 there were nearly four million. The vast majority lived in Georgia, Alabama, Tennessee, Mississippi, Arkansas, Louisiana, and Texas, the states known as the Cotton Belt.

Slaves in the Cotton Belt were treated more cruelly than ever. Lynching became a standard practice among paranoid slaveholders. White posses searched the homes of blacks, broke up black gatherings, and killed a black at the first hint of rebellion.

Cotton plantation owners kept increasing their slave holdings, either through illegal importation or legal and illegal interstate trade. Yet now they feared massive rebellion more than ever. They had reason to. It was obvious that the winds of change were blowing.

Resources

AFRICA: PAST AND PRESENT

Abrahams, Roger B. *African Folktales: Traditional Stories of the Black World.* **New York: Pantheon, 1983.**

A collection of folklore from different parts of Africa.

Appiah, Joseph. *Joe Appiah: The Life of an African Patriot.* **New York: Praeger, 1990.**

A detailed autobiography of one of the people instrumental in liberating Ghana from British control in 1957.

Brooks, George E. *Landlords and Strangers: Ecology, Society, and Trade in Western Africa, 1000–1630.* **Boulder, CO: Westview Press, 1993.**

Empires such as Songhay and Mali rose and fell with the business carried out along the ancient trade routes of West Africa. How did people from vastly different societies come around to making deals? What was the effect of trade on the land, and the land on the trade? These are some of the questions addressed in this book.

Chu, Daniel, and Skinner, Elliott. *A Glorious Age in Africa: The Story of Three Great African Empires.* **Garden City: Doubleday, 1965.**

Centuries ago, before the arrival of Europeans in Africa, three great empires rose and fell along the Niger River in West Africa. They traded with the forest peoples to the south as well as with the Arabs to the north, enjoying great power and prosperity. In this book, the stories of Ghana, Mali, and Songhay are set out in all their splendor.

Claridge, W. Walton. *A History of the Gold Coast and Ashanti.* **New York: Barnes & Noble, 1964.**

This two-volume work documents the history of the relationship between the Kingdom of Asante (Ashanti) and the British during the nineteenth century. Asante was the major regional power and controlled the gold trade. It resisted British domination until the very end of the century.

Colvin, Lucie Gallistel. *Historical Dictionary of Senegal*. Metuchen, NJ: Scarecrow Press, 1981.

A paragraph apiece on all the major places and players in the history of this West African republic. A few pages at the beginning are dedicated to a historical outline of Senegal, followed by a year-by-year chronology. A great reference for anyone interested in the history of Senegal.

Daaku, Kwame Yeboa. *Trade and Politics on the Gold Coast, 1600–1720: A Study of the African Reaction to European Trade*. London: Clarendon Press, 1970.

During the seventeenth century, the Fante were in control of the coastal trade in gold and slaves, acting as the middlemen between the Asante (Ashanti) and the British. This work outlines how the African societies changed as they prospered through trade with the Europeans.

Decalo, Samuel. *Historical Dictionary of Togo*. Metuchen, NJ: Scarecrow Press, 1976.

This small republic shares much of its precolonial history with its neighbors Ghana, Benin, and Burkina Faso, but its history in the last century is more distinct. All of the people and groups who played an important role in Togo's history are listed alphabetically.

Egwuonwu, Ani Dike. *Marriage Problems in Africa*. New York: Continental Services, 1986.

Exposure to elements of Western industrial society has threatened traditional African ways of life. Egwuonwu ably tackles the complicated and controversial issues surrounding marriage in modern Africa.

Elliott, Kit. *Benin*. Cambridge: Cambridge University Press, 1973.

The origins of the kingdom of Benin go back some 800 years. From the sixteenth to the nineteenth centuries, Benin (not to be confused with the modern republic) was the undisputed master of southern Nigeria. Conquered peoples hundreds of miles away owed tribute and allegiance to the Oba (king) of Benin. Take a look into its turbulent past, and into the beautiful capital, Benin City, where the Oba lives to this day.

Gailey, Harry A. *Historical Dictionary of the Gambia*. Metuchen, NJ: Scarecrow Press, 1975.

A great reference book that lists all the major players in Gambian history, whether they be Africans, Britons, whole ethnic groups, organizations, or even crops, in alphabetical order. It also includes a brief history and a year-by-year chronology.

Hatch, John Charles. *Africa: The Rebirth of Self-Rule*. London: Oxford University Press, 1967.

The independence of Ghana in 1957 was the beginning of the end of European colonialism in Africa. Read about how the evolving thinking of African intellectuals and politicians in the 1940s and '50s led to the explosion of new republics in the '60s.

Isichei, Elizabeth Allo. *A History of Nigeria*. New York: Longman, 1983.

It is difficult to get a grasp on the most populous country in Africa. Nigeria's 100 million people speak some 200 languages and are religiously split between Christianity, Islam, and traditional beliefs. Although Nigeria was always expected to race past the rest of Africa into prosperity, corrupt military governments have prevented it from reaching its full potential. A view of the country's history helps you begin to understand where Nigeria is now and where it is going.

——. *A History of the Igbo People.* **New York: St. Martin's Press, 1976.**

The Igbo of southeastern Nigeria are known for their traditional preference for democratic government over the monarchy espoused by their neighbors of the former Kingdom of Benin. The Igbo are the ancestors of many African Americans.

Jefferson, Margo. *Roots of Time: A Portrait of African Life and Culture.* **Garden City, NY: Zenith Books, 1974.**

Lovely photos adorn this book, which tries to give the reader a taste of the rich variety of cultures and lifestyles found on the African continent. Beliefs and rituals of selected groups concerning birth and childhood, marriage and family, religion, art, and other topics are presented and explained.

Jones, Constance. *Africa, 1500–1900.* **New York: Facts on File, 1993.**

With plenty of maps and illustrations, this is a short introduction to an important era in African history. In 1500, Africans had a great deal of control over the new trade with the Europeans; by 1900 the Europeans had consolidated their colonial claims over most of the continent.

Loth, Heinrich. *Woman of Ancient Africa.* **Westport, CT: L. Hill & Co., 1987.**

This book, translated from the German by Sheila Marnie, explores the roles of women in the more remote periods of African history, from ancient Nubia and Egypt to the great empires of West Africa.

Meyerowitz, Eva Lewin-Richter. *The Early History of the Akan States of Ghana.* **London: Red Candle Press, 1974.**

The able Meyerowitz untangles the complex and intriguing political history of the Akan, a group of peoples who include the Fante, Asante (Ashanti), and Twi. Read about their migrations, battles, and shifting alliances, their dealings with the Muslims and Europeans, and more. Meyerowitz's focus extends from about 1000 to 1750.

Mundt, Robert J. *Historical Dictionary of the Ivory Coast (Côte d'Ivoire).* **Metuchen, NJ: Scarecrow Press, 1987.**

The Ivory Coast gained its independence from France in 1960. This is an alphabetical listing of terms and political leaders important in this country's history, along with maps and a timeline of important events.

Owusu-Ansah, David, and McFarland, Daniel Miles. *Historical Dictionary of Ghana.* **Metuchen, NJ: Scarecrow Press, 1995.**

The people of Ghana are known for being shrewd businesspeople, for maintaining some of the longest resistance in all Africa to European colonialism, and for being the first to shake off that colonialism by becoming independent in 1957. But there's much more to their history than that. If you're reading a history of Ghana, have this handy reference at your side.

Oyewole, A. *Historical Dictionary of Nigeria.* **Metuchen, NJ: Scarecrow Press, 1987.**

Igbo, Yoruba, Nupe, Egba, Hausa, Fulani . . . sometimes the peoples of Nigeria seem to have moved about and interacted in a million different ways. How can you keep it all straight? A summary of Nigerian history, a year-by-year chronology, and an alphabetical list of all major historical figures, kingdoms, and forces are good ways to start. You'll find them all in this book.

Shaw, Thurstan. *Nigeria: Its Archaeology and Early History*. London: Thames and Hudson, 1978.

Oral history and origin myths of West African peoples give versions of their lands' ancient past and where the people who settled there came from. Modern archaeology and scholarship can add to this historical knowledge by uncovering and dating the remains of fallen empires.

Smith, Robert Sydney. *Kingdoms of the Yoruba*. London: Methuen, 1969.

The Yoruba are among the most famous and culturally influential peoples of Africa. They had several small kingdoms in southwestern Nigeria.

Stride, G. T., and Ifeka, Caroline. *Peoples and Empires of West Africa: West Africa in History, 1000– 1800*. New York: Africana Publishing Corp., 1971.

The 800 years covered in this history were a time of massive power struggles, astounding wealth, and flourishing culture in West Africa. The medieval glory of the Songhay, Mali, and Ghana empires was overtaken by the Benin, Dahomey, Asante (Ashanti), Nupe, and others during the first centuries of trade with Europe.

Turnbull, Colin M. *Man in Africa*. Newton Abbot, U.K.: David & Charles, 1976.

This illustrated book documents the history of the human presence in Africa. It includes much information on the customs of the various African ethnic groups.

Ume, Kalu E. *The Rise of British Colonialism in Southern Nigeria, 1700–1900*. Smithtown, NY: Exposition Press, 1980.

The Yoruba, Igbo, and Edo all traded with the British for centuries. Eventually, however, they all fell to British might. Discover the causes that turned ancient, proud societies into vassals.

Vlahos, Olivia. *African Beginnings*. **New York: Viking Press, 1967.**

A comprehensive and engaging cultural history of Africa is derived from the extensive work of archaeologists and anthropologists. Illustrator George Ford skillfully recreates scenes of African life throughout history.

Vollmer, Jurgen. *Black Genesis: African Roots.* **New York: St. Martin's Press, 1980.**

Follow in the footsteps of Kunta Kinte, the star of Alex Haley's *Roots*. Jurgen Vollmer has photographed the landscape from Kinte's childhood home, the Mandingo village of Juffure, to Dakar, Senegal, the port from which he was shipped to the United States. John Devere's text accompanies Vollmer's breathtaking and moving photography.

Wepman, Dennis. *Africa: The Struggle for Independence*. **New York: Facts on File, 1993.**

Throughout the twentieth century, Africans worked and strove to achieve independence for their recently conquered societies. Read about the people who, sometimes peacefully, sometimes violently, made the dream of self-determination a reality.

Wilks, Ivor. *Forests of Gold: Essays on the Akan and the Kingdom of Asante*. **Athens: Ohio University Press, 1993.**

Enlightening essays on the Akan, a group of peoples including the Fante, Asante, and Twi in what is now Ghana. Wilks focuses on the Kingdom of Asante (Ashanti), which rose to dominate the region in the early 1700s and prospered by trading gold with the Europeans until its defeat at the hands of the British in the 1880s.

THE SLAVE TRADE

Artemel, Janice; Crowell, Elizabeth A.; and Parker, Jeff. *The Alexandria Slave Pen: The Archeology of*

Urban Captivity. Washington, DC: Engineering-Science, Inc., 1987.

> Slavery has existed for thousands of years. These authors study the many eras and places where this institution was practiced and compare the societies' attitudes, purposes, and treatment of their slaves.

Bean, Richard Nelson. *The British Trans-Atlantic Slave Trade, 1650–1775*. New York: Arno Press, 1975.

> The British engaged in the trade in human beings to supply cheap labor for their colonies in America, which stretched from Maine to Guyana. What the African traders gained in profit, they lost in human resources and in their own spirit. Find out how this horrid business was carried out.

Curtin, Philip D., ed. *Africa Remembered: Narratives by West Africans from the Era of the Slave Trade*. Madison: University of Wisconsin Press, 1967.

> The editor has compiled from various parts of West Africa a wealth of oral tradition that has survived from the time of the slave trade. In this way he presents to the reader the African point of view on this contentious issue.

Davidson, Basil. *The African Slave Trade*. Boston: Little, Brown, 1980.

> This is a serious economic study of the slave trade and its profitability for African, European, and American traders. It details changes in agricultural practices, attitudes, and laws that affected this major world market.

Du Bois, W. E. B. *The Suppression of African Slave-Trade to the United States of America*. New York: Social Science Press, 1954.

> A law was passed in 1807, taking effect on January 1, 1808, that made it illegal to import slaves to the United States. This law was the culmination of decades of power

struggles among various factions. Even after the law had taken effect, states in the Deep South were still attempting to repeal it.

Duignan, Peter, and Gann, L. H. *The United States and Africa: A History*. Cambridge: Cambridge University Press, 1984.

America was economically involved with Africa throughout the nineteenth century. Beginning with American participation in the slave trade, this book goes on to discuss the 1800 war between the United States and the Barbary Pirates (an Arab group in North Africa) and the repatriation of ex-slaves to Liberia and Sierra Leone after the Civil War.

Howard, Warren S. *American Slavers and the Federal Law, 1837–1862*. Berkeley: University of California Press, 1963.

The law, effective 1808, that prohibited the importation of slaves made criminals of many ship captains and slave traders. Ships continued to sail to Africa and the Caribbean to buy slaves, then secretly sell them to traders on the U.S. coast. This book tells about the effort made to catch and punish those guilty of this federal crime.

Law, Robin. *The Slave Coast of West Africa, 1550–1750: The Impact of the Atlantic Slave Trade on an African Society*. Oxford: Clarendon Press; New York: Oxford University Press, 1991.

The Slave Coast was the name given to the territory occupied by the Yoruba, Ewe, and other groups because of the large numbers of slaves purchased there. This book outlines how centuries of fomenting war to acquire captives for sale physically and spiritually affected the Africans who sold slaves.

SLAVERY AND SLAVE LIFE

Blacks Who Stole Themselves: Advertisements for Runaways in the Pennsylvania Gazette, *1728–1790*. Philadelphia: University of Pennsylvania Press, 1980.

Pennsylvania was one of the better places for a slave to try escape. It was full of Moravians and Quakers whose religious objections to slavery led them to help slaves consistently for over a century. The reward money offered in these ads indicates what the runaway slaves were worth to the owners.

Blassingame, John W. *The Slave Community*. New York: Oxford University Press, 1972.

Ripped from their territory, cut off from their families, forbidden to speak their own language, treated like pack animals, African slaves in America had to find ways to continue with their lives under adverse circumstances. One way was to form strong communities with other slaves. A rich culture and feeling of racial unity grew from these bonds.

Campbell, Edward D. C., and Rice, Kym S., eds. *Before Freedom Came: African-American Life in the Antebellum South*. Richmond, VA: Museum of the Confederacy, 1991.

Contributors' essays cover topics such as the lives of plantation slaves, the experiences of female slaves, and black life in the cities of the old South. Illustrated with rare engravings, photographs, and maps.

Douglass, Frederick. *Frederick Douglass, in His Own Words*. San Diego: Harcourt Brace Jovanovich, 1995.

Excerpts from Douglass's speeches are chosen to give an insight into the sort of person he was. This is a fine introduction to Douglass's complete speeches and writings.

Katz, William Loren. *Breaking the Chains: African American Slave Resistance*. New York: Atheneum, 1990.

Blacks were not passive about slavery. This book documents slave revolts in Southern states between 1775 and 1865. The exodus of blacks to the north to fight in the Civil War is also documented.

McGarry, Howard, and Lawson, Bill E. *Between Slavery and Freedom: Philosophy and American Slavery.* **Bloomington: Indiana University Press, 1992.**

The late eighteenth and early nineteenth centuries in Europe and the United States were characterized by the idea that any problem could be solved with the correct application of reason. This book shows how both slavery's supporters and its opponents tried to use classical Greek and Christian philosophy to bolster their stand on the issue.

Paulson, Timothy J. *Days of Sorrow, Years of Glory, 1831–1850: From the Nat Turner Revolt to the Fugitive Slave Law.* **New York: Chelsea House, 1994.**

This is a historical look at the period between two major events in the history of American slavery. Nat Turner led a slave revolt that came the closest to success of any to occur in the United States. In contrast to those heady days of possibility, the Fugitive Slave Law allowed slave owners to try to capture escaped slaves even in the Northern states where slavery was outlawed.

Rawick, George P., ed. *The American Slave: A Composite Autobiography.* **Westport, CT: Greenwood Publishing, 1972.**

By combining elements of the experiences of various slaves as recorded in their autobiographical tales and stories, the editor has presented the autobiography of an imaginary slave who symbolizes the plight of all the men and women who suffered under the institution.

White, Anne Terry. *Human Cargo: The Story of the Atlantic Slave Trade.* **Champaign, IL: Garrard, 1972.**

The gruesome history of slaving is told through eyewitness accounts in this book for young readers. The relationships of West Africa to the American South are explained, along with the inspiring tale of the long struggle for abolition.

Chapter 3
Freedom and the African Cultural Diaspora

By the end of the eighteenth century, opposition to slavery was beginning to grow in Britain's colonies in the West Indies. The abolitionists there started societies that pushed for an end to slavery. Although there was not much strong sentiment against slavery among the people living in Britain, the voice of the colonists was heard across the ocean. In 1838, Britain freed all the slaves in its colonies and made them citizens.

This decision made in far-away London was not without effect in the United States. Slaveholders were aware that the change in moral outlook that caused the British decision could occur in the United States. The abolitionist movement there was already beginning to pick up steam.

American abolitionists were a varied group, including whites as well as blacks, Southerners as well as Northerners. Many of the white women who were abolitionists were also supporters of women suffrage. They recognized that racial bigotry and sexist bigotry were both unjust expressions of inequality and that all such inequalities should be eradicated. Black abolitionists included orators Sojourner Truth, a woman who later argued for women's suffrage; Frederick Douglass, a former slave who escaped to the North and began his activism writing articles and pamphlets; and Harriet Tubman, who helped establish the Underground Railroad, a network of safehouses all over the eastern United States. Escaped slaves found shelter, food, and assistance on their way to freedom in Canada. The black ministers Charles Lenox Redmond and Henry Highland Garnet represented another aspect of abolitionism. They were less interested in the moral or humanitarian aspects of ending slavery

Abolitionist Harriet Tubman (far left) helped to establish the Underground Railroad, a network of people who helped slaves escape to freedom in Canada.

than with getting the job done. The priority in their militant campaign was to encourage the formation of armed, trained black militias to eradicate slavery by force if necessary. Among white abolitionists were many passionate spirits, and often vehement infighting occurred because of differences within the ranks. The American Anti-Slavery Society believed that slavery could be dismantled only gradually. This angered people like William Lloyd Garrison, who so keenly felt the moral outrage of slavery that to them anything other than immediate abolition was like a deal with the devil.

Throughout the middle of the nineteenth century the American people wrangled over the future of the Africans among them. There were battles in Congress, where a Southern senator beat a New England abolitionist senator almost to death on the Senate floor. There were battles among the populace; in the months leading up to a referendum on slavery in the new state of Kansas, bloody battles were fought between the two sides. Illinois Senator Abraham

Lincoln believed that the union of the states could not be maintained with the slavery question unsettled, and he came down on the side of abolition. When he was elected president in 1860, South Carolina took matters into its own hands and seceded from the United States.

South Carolina firmly believed that slavery, as well as other issues, were questions best decided by the people of each state, and it seceded from the Union. Eventually ten other states followed South Carolina's lead: Virginia, North Carolina, Georgia, Florida, Tennessee, Alabama, Mississippi, Arkansas, Louisiana, and Texas. Together they formed the Confederate States of America. The remaining states wanted to reunite the Union and were opposed to slavery. A battle between Union troops and a South Carolina militia in 1861 sparked civil war. Remarkably, some Southern whites turned to slaves to help them fight for Southern rights. Some did, reluctantly. The majority of blacks fought in the Union Army. Four years later the war ended in the defeat of the Confederate States and the restoration of the Union.

The twelve years after the Civil War, 1865 to 1877, are called *Reconstruction*. The war caused great devastation in the South—physical, social, and economic—and the idea was that it needed to be "reconstructed." The social reconstruction included the integration of African Americans into the society from which they had always been excluded.

The first steps toward that integration were taken with President Lincoln's Emancipation Proclamation in 1863. But the slaves could not really exercise their freedom until the war was over. When they learned that they were free, many of them lost all feeling of connection to the plantation where they had worked the years away for nothing. Many left with their families and hit the road, simply because they could for the first time in their lives. At first the freedmen tended to wander about with no particular destination in mind. Later, however, more and more headed toward Southern cities and towns.

For those who stayed in the countryside, the most important issue of the time was land ownership. Although blacks had achieved freedom and citizenship by law, only land ownership provided real social and economic independence in an agricultural society like the American South. Union General William T. Sherman seemed to realize this. Early in 1865, before the war was quite over, he set aside a strip of Formerly Confederate land for freedmen on the Atlantic Ocean, from Charleston, South Carolina, to Jacksonville, Florida, extending thirty miles inland. By the middle of the year, some 40,000 African American settlers had staked out their claims. But President Andrew Johnson and others in Washington were not committed to granting blacks true freedom through land ownership. At the end of 1865, the previous owners of this strip of land had begun to return and successfully reclaim their property.

The following year another attempt was made to provide land to African Americans. Land that the U.S. government owned in Florida, Alabama, Mississippi, Arkansas, and Missouri was made available to the public. Many blacks took advantage of this opportunity to become landowners.

Every now and then during Reconstruction, opportunities arose in the South that encouraged blacks to own a plot of land that they could farm, so that they would be less likely to be dependent on others for food. The federal government established the Bureau of Refugees, Freedmen, and Abandoned Lands. With limited resources, they attempted to ease the transition of African Americans from slaves to free Americans. By 1870, however, only five percent of southern blacks were landowners.

The Reconstruction era was also the first time most blacks were allowed to vote in the United States. African Americans were encouraged to register and vote during these years. As a result, several Southern states including South Carolina and Mississippi had blacks in their legislatures. In Louisiana, two of seven officers who led state government were black. Some black politicians made it as far as the U.S. House of Representatives.

But most of the benefits the freedmen received in these years, many of which were imposed by the Union, vanished when Reconstruction ended in 1877. The Southerners enacted laws that reintroduced and enforced racial segregation in the public and private realms. The newly won right to vote was severely curtailed or taken away from blacks altogether. The practice of lynching, in which vigilante mobs hunted and murdered African Americans for real or imagined offenses, became more and more common.

The sharecropping system of agriculture symbolized the obstacles Southern blacks faced as they tried to improve their lives. The owner of a farm would get one or more black families to work the farm and keep it going. In return the families could live on the property and receive a percentage of the farm's profit at the end of the year. If a worker required tools or extra food, he bought them on credit from the farm owner. But at year's end, it was not uncommon for the owner to be dishonest about settling the accounts. The sharecropping system tied African Americans as tightly to the land as slavery did.

Black land ownership in the South did increase during the decades following Reconstruction. By 1900, 14 percent of African American farmers in Georgia owned the land they farmed. In Virginia, the figure was as high as 59 percent. But sharecropping was the principal way of life for most blacks for about sixty years.

One way that African Americans tried to better their lives was by moving. In fact, migration out of the South was a major part of the African American experience for almost a century after Reconstruction ended. The first major movement headed toward the West. Black leader Benjamin "Pap" Singleton understood that blacks would achieve freedom only through land ownership. As more and more were crossing the Mississippi in search of a new life, Singleton saw a chance to join them and resettle African Americans on land of their own. In 1879 he set his sights on Kansas and organized people all over the South. Some 40,000 followed him out to the prairies. At first the whites in Kansas welcomed the newcomers. But as their numbers began to swell, the whites began to disapprove. In the end, most of Singleton's

Freed slaves faced social and economic barriers to land ownership. Many, like these peanut pickers in Virginia in the late 1890s, found themselves still working for white farm owners.

followers returned to the South. But the trend of westward movement continued at a slow but steady pace over the next few decades.

The second major wave of migration, movement to the Northern cities, was sparked by World War I, which lasted from 1914 to 1918. The war helped bring African Americans from South to North in four ways. 1) It made emigration to the United States almost impossible for Europeans. They were either fighting in the war, or were forbidden to cross international boundaries. So the growing industries in the North were not getting the workers they needed from Europe. Southern blacks partly filled this labor gap. 2) It caused the production of manufactured goods from Europe to drop substantially, as factories contributed hardware to the war effort. Thus American factories needed more workers to meet the world's higher demand for American manufactured goods. Once again, many of these new workers were African Americans from the South. 3) When the

The Wild West attracted many African Americans, who saw the South as a breeding ground for racism and injustice. Some African Americans, like Nat Love of South Dakota, even became cowboys.

United States entered the war in 1917, most of the people who crossed the ocean to fight were white male workers. Their spots on the assembly lines were often taken by Southern blacks. 4) When African Americans did go to fight in the war in Europe, the Armed Forces were segregated, so they fought in all-black regiments. This gave them a chance to meet people from other walks of life. The Tennessee sharecropper learned about life in the North from the Chicago factory worker and thought that maybe starting out fresh in the North would be better for his kids. The Philadelphia teacher heard about the humiliation suffered by his Georgia sharecropper comrade and told him that if he ever wanted to come to Philly, he'd have a place to stay.

Although conditions in the Northern cities were often better than in the Southern cotton fields, African Americans did not entirely escape their troubles. Just like the Kansans forty years earlier, the Northern city dwellers became more intolerant of the new arrivals as their numbers grew. Tensions escalated and peaked in the summer of 1919, called "Red Summer." Cities across the country saw violence against blacks rise to ghastly proportions that year. Still blacks immigrated north.

When people made the move North, they tended to go more or less straight north. People from Florida, Georgia, and the Carolinas usually ended up in Washington, Baltimore, Philadelphia, New York, or Boston. People from Mississippi, Arkansas, and Alabama headed toward Chicago, St. Louis, Detroit, or Milwaukee. The route from the "Delta"—the cotton-growing area of northwestern Mississippi—to Chicago was one of the more heavily traveled. Both a road and a railway line ran directly from the Delta to the Windy City. During and after the war, Chicago's black-owned newspaper, the *Defender*, made a concerted effort to lure Southerners with articles trumpeting the higher wages and relative prosperity of the African Americans already there. So many people heeded the call of the *Defender* that a labor shortage hit the Delta in the 1920s and '30s. In Mississippi and other parts of the South, frightened farm owners

Resentment of the large numbers of African American migrants to Chicago in the early twentieth century resulted in race riots in the summer of 1919. Above, police officers watch as a man moves his belongings to a "safety zone" during the riots. Violence erupted in cities around the country during what was known as "Red Summer."

banned the *Defender*, throwing into jail people who sold it, as well as agents from Chicago who were suspected of encouraging people to leave the fields.

Nevertheless, the rate of African American migration from South to North only increased. The invention of a mechanical cotton-picking machine in 1944 meant that far fewer people were needed to work the Southern cotton farms. At the same time, the end of World War II the next year meant more bombed-out factories in Europe and more growth opportunities for American manufacturers in Northern cities. Five million blacks left the South between 1940 and 1970; the Chicago blues music scene of the 1950s and '60s is almost entirely a product of musicians who arrived from the Delta after World War II. Still more left home for Southern cities like Atlanta and Houston. Today, only half of African Americans live in the South (compared with three-quarters in 1940), while one in seven African Americans lives in rural areas (compared with half in 1940).

In the 1950s and '60s, many immigrants began coming from the Caribbean. The people in this early group tended to be well educated and highly skilled, and most rose to the upper middle classes rather quickly. Since then the numbers have been growing. Haiti and the Dominican Republic, both countries with a very high percentage of Africans, are among the top ten nations in number of immigrants arriving in the United States. It has been common for Caribbeans to emigrate to Great Britain; many of the islands, such as Trinidad and Jamaica, are former British colonies. But some of these émigrés have later emigrated to the United States as the economy in Britain slowed. The number of people coming directly from Africa is still relatively small, but in each decade since 1970 twice as many arrived as had in the previous decade.

The African Cultural Diaspora

When people go to live in a new place and amid a new culture, they do not leave their home behind entirely. Generations and centuries of customs and traditions die hard. Rather than disappear completely, they are more likely to be changed and adapted by the displaced group. Africans who were forcibly taken to the Americas lost much of their cultural identity when they left their land for good, but they retained elements that are still around to this day.

The spread and adaptation of African traditional arts and language to other places and times is known as the cultural diaspora. Remarkable examples of African cultural adaptation are found among the Gullah, a group of people living on the Sea Islands, off the coast of Georgia and South Carolina. The Gullah have retained perhaps more evidence of their African ancestry than any other African American community. Their language is a mixture of African and English words. A Gullah often has two distinct given names: one that appears on her birth certificate, and a nickname known only to others in the community. Gullah nicknames often sound like English nicknames, but researchers have discovered that they are actually of African origin, modified to sound like English names the Gullah heard around them. Another cultural trait the Gullah retained from Africa is the concept of family. The principal family unit among many whites in America is the nuclear family (father, mother, and siblings). Among the Gullah, one's "family" is one's extended family, including grandparents, aunts, uncles, and cousins. This idea can also be found in many societies in Africa. African traces are even apparent in the way the Gullah design and build their homes.

All over the Americas, Africans and their descendants have held onto at least some aspect of their home. The most obvious example of this cultural adaptation is African music. Slaves were forbidden to play the drums when they found themselves in America, but they retained many memories of the West African talking drum, *kpegisu*, *kora*, and other instruments. Wherever Africans went in the Americas, new musical forms were born of the fusion between these memories and the European music they heard. Gospel, blues, country, ragtime, jazz, rock 'n' roll, soul, R & B, funk, and hip-hop are some of the varied ways in which African Americans have expressed themselves musically in their new surroundings. Salsa, samba, and reggae are examples of musical traditions with African roots that developed in the Caribbean and South America. All of these forms have since become part of the mainstream culture in the United States. In fact, since the radio was invented, Americans have rarely been able to turn it on without hearing African-based music.

The cultural diaspora is also evident in popular dance forms. From African traditional dance forms came the very idea of swiveling, pulsing, and jutting hips, shoulders, and heads to strong rhythms. European-based dance forms, traditional and otherwise, do not feature the same kinds and combinations of movement. Even American ballroom dance has movements traceable to West African peoples. Rhythm tap dance, a type of dance related to improvisational jazz drumming, is making a comeback. It has its roots in African drumming patterns; when slaves were not allowed to use drums, they used their feet to make the intricate rhythms of their ancestral land.

The Gullah people of South Carolina have displayed amazing resiliency in maintaining African traditions. Ralph Fripp, a resident of St. Helena Island, weaves shrimp nets and still speaks the Gullah language.

In worship and in everyday language, in family relationships, in music and in dance, the descendants of the Africans who were brought to the Americas so long ago retain much of the culture of their ancestors. In this way, black communities today, from Canada to Brazil, have maintained a link with the Africa of their forebears. Researching a family history is a way for you to discover your personal link with Africa.

Resources

FREE BLACKS AND FREEDMEN

Handler, Jerome S. *The Unappropriated People: Freedmen in the Slave Society of Barbados.* **Baltimore: Johns Hopkins University Press, 1974.**

Barbados is an island in the West Indies, formerly owned by Great Britain. Most blacks there were slaves, but some were freed by their masters. This book tells how these people got by, in between the ranks of the white slaveowners and their enslaved fellow blacks.

Oubre, Claude F. *Forty Acres and a Mule: The Freedmen's Bureau and Black Land Ownership.* **Baton Rouge: Louisiana State University Press, 1978.**

During Reconstruction, a rumor ran rampant through the South. The Freedmen's Bureau, a government agency created to help freed slaves, was going to *give* forty acres of land and a mule to every black family. This rumor proved to be unfounded, and land ownership became a tricky prize for African Americans to snare.

West, Richard. *Back to Africa: A History of Sierra Leone and Liberia.* **New York: Holt, Rinehart and Winston, 1971.**

In the early nineteenth century, many free African Americans sailed to these two West African countries to live as free people in a black society. Read their story in West's illustrated book.

Wilson, Carol. *Freedom at Risk: The Kidnapping of Free Blacks in America, 1780–1865.* **Lexington: University Press of Kentucky, 1994.**

Throughout the slavery era in America there were always a significant number of free blacks, mostly in the North, but in the South as well. But as long as their kinsmen were in bondage, they could never be certain of their own safety. This book unearths hard-to-find evidence that free blacks were kidnapped and sold into slavery, while very few were willing to come to their aid.

RECONSTRUCTION AND MODERN HISTORY

African Diaspora Studies Newsletter. **Washington, DC: Howard University Press.**

This journal, in publication since 1984, focuses on artistic and political developments of interest to the African American community. Issues such as civil rights and modern immigration receive commentary from the faculty and students of Howard University, as well as other experts.

Branch, Taylor. *Parting the Waters: America in the King Years, 1954–1963*. New York: Simon & Schuster, 1988.

This is a thorough examination of the beginnings of the modern civil rights movement, placed in the larger picture of American society and politics. It's a big project at 1,000 pages, but there is perhaps no better or more comprehensive history of this crucial era.

Dennis, R. Ethel. *The Black People of America.* New Haven: Readers Press, 1970.

Africans and their descendants have been living in the United States for almost 400 years. This book documents their struggles and triumphs, and the rich and vibrant culture they have developed through it all.

Feagin, Joe R., and Feagin, Clairece Booher. *Discrimination American Style: Institutional Racism and Sexism.* Englewood Cliffs, NJ: Prentice-Hall, 1978.

A discussion of the nature of discrimination in the United States and of the civil rights movement and affirmative action programs.

Harris, Joseph, ed. *Global Dimensions of the African Diaspora*. Washington, DC: Howard University, 1982.

It is important to remember that the diaspora of African culture has not affected the United States alone. This is a consideration of how African-rooted ideas have spread throughout the world and how other nations have been indirectly influenced by watching diaspora developments in the Americas.

Harvey, James C. *Black Civil Rights During the Johnson Administration*. Jackson: University and College Press of Mississippi, 1973.

Harvey's book documents the strides made in civil rights for African Americans during the presidency of Lyndon Johnson, 1963–1969. Malcolm X and Martin Luther King, Jr., lived and died during this period.

Holloway, Joseph, E., ed. *Africanisms in American Culture*. Bloomington: Indiana University Press, 1990.

An Africanism is a cultural element of African origin. This book reminds us that many African American cultural developments have found their way into the broader American culture, from the music on the radio to the Negro spirituals sung in Catholic churches.

Hornsby, Alton, Jr., ed. *In the Cage: Eyewitness Accounts of the Freed Negro in Southern Society, 1877–1929*. Chicago: Quadrangle Books, 1971.

The author takes the position that American white society's concept of blacks at the turn of the century can best be understood in its own words. To this end he has compiled selections from letters, diaries, and other documents by whites who interacted with or witnessed African American life in urban and rural areas.

Hudson, Barbara A. *Facing the Rising Sun: 150 Years of the African-American Experience, 1842–1992.* **Hartford, CT: Wadsworth Atheneum, 1993.**

This is the catalog of an exhibition held in Hartford. With pamphlets, film footage, newspaper clippings, drawings, and other artifacts, the exhibition documented and celebrated the last 150 years of African American history.

Irwin, Graham. *Africans Abroad.* **New York: Columbia University Press, 1977.**

This is a history of the black diaspora in Asia, Latin America, and the Caribbean during the age of slavery. It is interesting to focus on the earliest centuries of the diaspora, and to consider how different cultures were affected by the new influences from Africa.

Katz, William Loren. *Black Indians: A Hidden Heritage.* **New York: Atheneum, 1986.**

African Americans and Native Americans were in a similar social situation in the seventeenth century, working as servants or slaves for whites or shunted off to special neighborhoods and reserves. This mutual sympathy sometimes led to unions and to children. This book explores this unusual angle of genealogy.

———. *Black People Who Made the Old West.* **New York: Crowell, 1977.**

The cowboys and pioneers of the American West were little like their portrayal in movies and some history books. People of all backgrounds and nationalities herded cattle and worked the land. Thousands of these people were black. Written for a young audience, this book offers short biographies of thirty-five black frontiersmen and -women.

Novak, Daniel A. *The Wheel of Servitude: Black Forced Labor After Slavery.* **Lexington: University Press of Kentucky, 1978.**

The four million blacks who were released from slavery after the Civil War did not all find access to education and good jobs. Many—homeless, penniless, illiterate, and without skills—were forced into an exploitative labor situation not unlike the slavery from which they had supposedly just been freed.

Nuñez, Benjamin. *Dictionary of Afro-Latin American Civilization.* **Westport, CT: Greenwood, 1980.**

In the seventeenth century black slaves began coming to North America from the West Indies and South America. Since then this ethnic group has developed a unique culture that blends African, Hispanic, and North American elements.

Toplin, Robert Brent. *The Legacy of Slavery in the United States and Brazil.* **Westport, CT: Greenwood Press, 1981.**

When slavery was abolished, its centuries-long history did not evaporate. The echoes of forced servitude still haunt the slave-owning Americas in aspects of economics, culture, and race relations.

West, Cornel. *Race Matters.* **Boston: Beacon Press, 1993.**

This best-selling book discusses the current state of race relations in the United States. West believes that if the ideal of a radical democratic society were reawakened and the country's citizens actively participated in their own legislation, it would go a long way toward easing racial tensions.

SUCCESS STORIES

Angelou, Maya. *I Know Why the Caged Bird Sings.* **New York: Random House, 1969.**

Essayist, poet, and short-story writer Maya Angelou began life in rural poverty. These tales of her early years include such traumas as incest and unwanted pregnancy but still communicate her love of life and pride in her black roots.

Astor, Gerald. *"And a Credit to His Race": The Hard Life and Times of Joseph Louis Barrow, aka Joe Louis.* **New York: Saturday Review Press, 1974.**

When Joe Louis won a fight, it was symbolic to every African American within earshot of a radio: blacks were finally proving their strength. Louis's life in general was symbolic of that of millions of blacks. He rose from poverty through hard work and talent, but even at the top he faced threats and racism.

Beaton, Margaret. *Oprah Winfrey, TV Talk Show Host.* **Chicago: Children's Press, 1990.**

Oprah Winfrey enters the homes of millions of Americans every weekday as the reigning queen of the burgeoning talk-show business. She's come a long way from her childhood on a farm in Mississippi.

Bentley, Judith. *Harriet Tubman.* **New York: F. Watts, 1990.**

This courageous former slave was a founder of the Underground Railroad, through which she helped thousands of fugitive slaves to safety. She was also instrumental in assisting Northern forces during the Civil War.

Coffey, Wayne R. *Carl Lewis.* **Woodbridge, CT: Blackbirch Press, 1993.**

Carl Lewis is an African American track star. He has won prizes for short-distance running in most of the major world competitions, including Olympic medals in 1984, 1988, and 1992.

Darby, Jean. *Martin Luther King, Jr.* **Minneapolis: Lerner Publications, 1989.**

This Baptist minister became a hero to millions. King's inspiring leadership during the civil rights movement, as he preached the power of peaceful marches and demonstrations, was ended with his assassination in 1968.

Dyson, Michael Eric. *Making Malcolm: The Myth and Meaning of Malcolm X.* **New York: Oxford University Press, 1994.**

Malcolm X was a great civil rights leader who was assassinated in 1965. Although he is best remembered for his militant approach to black empowerment (the expression "By any means necessary" is his), after his pilgrimage to Mecca and his conversion to Islam he harbored a greater hope for a unified humanity.

Grier, Rosey. *All-American Heroes.* **New York: Master Media, 1993.**

The famed football player of the 1970s has written a dozen short biographies of African Americans of today, including comedian Bill Cosby, filmmaker Spike Lee, and television talk-show host Oprah Winfrey.

Grupenhoff, Richard. *The Black Valentino: The Stage and Screen Career of Lorenzo Tucker.* **Metuchen, NJ: Scarecrow, 1988.**

Lorenzo Tucker had all the virility and charm of Denzel Washington and Danny Glover. Unfortunately, the fact that this African American worked during the 1930s severely limited his access to stardom. His fame came from appearances in all-black Broadway reviews and as the male heartthrob in black independent films.

Halasa, Malu. *Mary McLeod Bethune.* **New York: Chelsea House, 1989.**

A fair opportunity for schooling has not always been available to African American young people. Mary McLeod Bethune's career-long fight for equality in education and political representation has been a major contribution to the future of America.

Haley, Alex. *Roots.* **Garden City: Doubleday, 1976.**

This is the most famous African American genealogy in the world, and the most fascinating. It inspired a generation of blacks to search for their connections with the past and taught this country about some of the realities of slavery.

Haskins, James. *Thurgood Marshall: A Life for Justice.* **New York: H. Holt, 1992.**

Marshall started his career as a lawyer and was very active in the civil rights movement in the 1950s. He spent the last decades of his long career as the first African American judge appointed to the U.S. Supreme Court.

Haskins, Jim, and Mitgang, N. R. *Mr. Bojangles: The Biography of Bill Robinson.* **New York: William Morrow, 1988.**

Bill Robinson was one of the first African American film superstars. He was beloved the world over for his great showmanship, beautiful dancing, and charitable spirit. This is his story.

Herbert, Solomon J., and Hill, George H. *Bill Cosby, Entertainer.* **New York: Chelsea House, 1991.**

From struggling stand-up comedian to prime-time TV star, Bill Cosby has always celebrated his roots. Through his long career he has challenged African American stereotypes and encouraged blacks to take pride in who they are.

Horne, Lena, and Schickel, Richard. *Lena.* **New York: Limelight, 1986.**

Since she burst on the Hollywood scene in the 1930s, Lena Horne has been beloved as a brilliant interpreter of show tunes and jazz standards. In this book she tells of the pride, self-doubt, discrimination, and triumph she felt during her first decades in the movies.

Johnson, Linda Carlson. *Barbara Jordan, Congresswoman.* **New York: Blackbirch Press/Rosen Publishing Group, 1990.**

> Barbara Jordan had three strikes against her at the start of her career: She was a black woman in the South. Discrimination could not stop her from becoming a lawyer and moving on to a political career. She later became a legislator for the state of Texas, and eventually a U.S. congresswoman.

King, Coretta Scott. *My Life with Martin Luther King, Jr.* **New York: H. Holt, 1993.**

> Coretta Scott King is the widow of the great civil rights leader. Here she tells young readers about the joys and heartbreak of working alongside a man who moved millions of people: some to enlightenment, some to rage.

Mandela, Nelson. *Long Walk to Freedom: The Autobiography of Nelson Mandela.* **Boston: Little, Brown, 1994.**

> A lengthy and informative autobiography of South Africa's current president, the first black to hold the position. Read about his education, the factors and conditions that led him to activism, his long imprisonment, and his release and rise to power.

May, Chris. *Bob Marley.* **London: H. Hamilton, 1985.**

> This influential Jamaican musician of the sixties and seventies brought reggae music out of Jamaica and onto the world scene. Marley continues to inspire people today and is something of a hero in Jamaica more than ten years after his death.

Patterson, Alex. *Spike Lee.* **New York: Avon Books, 1992.**

> The most famous black film director working today, Spike Lee was one of the first people to tell truly African Ameri-

can stories, from the black point of view, to a mass American audience. The director comments on his early films, his choice of subjects, and other aspects of his career.

Rambeck, Richard. *Patrick Ewing*. Mankato, MN: Child's World, 1994.

Patrick Ewing plays hoops for the New York Knicks. In this profile for young people he talks about his sport, his fame, his family, and life in New York for an African American with Caribbean roots.

Rennert, Richard, ed. *Book of Firsts: Sports Heroes*. New York: Chelsea House, 1994.

Many of the greatest stars in sports are African Americans. The record-holding athletes celebrated in this collection include Arthur Ashe, Jackie Robinson, Althea Gibson, and Jesse Owens.

Robeson, Paul. *Here I Stand*. New York: Othello Associates, 1958.

There have been few more remarkable people than Paul Robeson. Actor, singer, intellectual, political theorist, and cosmopolitan, his life successes and accomplishments are even more astonishing considering the racial discrimination he faced.

Robeson, Susan. *The Whole World in His Hands*. Secaucus, NJ: Citadel, 1981.

This is a loving portrait of Paul Robeson by his daughter, published only five years after his death. It features photographs from the family's private collection, as well as lucid commentary on some of the more controversial events in Robeson's life. Among the most famous of those are several race riots that occurred during concerts he gave in Peekskill, New York, in 1949.

Rose, Phyllis. *Jazz Cleopatra: Josephine Baker in Her Time*. New York: Doubleday, 1989.

The great singer and dancer Josephine Baker lived from 1906 to 1975. Those were years rife with change for African Americans. Baker herself coped with discrimination partly by spending a large part of her career in France. This biography of a gifted and brave life includes an interesting comparison of racial issues at the time in America and France.

Stafford, Mark. *W. E. B. Du Bois*. New York: Chelsea House, 1989.

Stafford's biography for young people examines the life of the great American scholar who dedicated his life to working for social justice for African Americans.

Washington, Margaret, ed. *The Narrative of Sojourner Truth*. New York: Vintage Books, 1993.

Originally published in 1884, this is a fine edition of the biography of one of America's most vigorous social reformers. Born into slavery and later freed, Truth concentrated her efforts first on the abolition of slavery, then on women's rights, before her death in 1883.

Wolfe, Rinna. *Charles Richard Drew, M.D.* New York: F. Watts, 1991.

This is a biography for young readers about an important African American medical scientist. Dr. Drew invented a superior method of blood transfusion, using only the plasma rather than whole blood.

MODERN IMMIGRATION

Apraku, Kofi Konadu. *African Emigrés in the United States: A Missing Link in Africa's Social and Economic Development*. New York: Praeger, 1991.

In the last thirty years there has been a major increase in the number of African immigrants to the United States. A large percentage of these are educated, or are seeking education here. The author proposes that this exodus has drained intellectual blood from Africa, robbing her of potential leaders.

Dominguez, Virginia R. *From Neighbor to Stranger: The Dilemma of Caribbean Peoples in the United States.* **New Haven, CT: Antilles Research Program, Yale University, 1975.**

It is not only racism and unemployment that immigrants from the Caribbean must contend with. A large element of social shock comes from being accustomed to a tightly knit community and having to make a new home in a society that does not always take the idea of community so much to heart.

Levine, Barry B., ed. *The Caribbean Exodus.* **New York: Praeger, 1987.**

This is a good introduction to the social, political, and economic reasons behind the great outpouring of Caribbean émigrés in the last fifty years.

Maingot, Anthony P., ed. *Small Country Development and International Labor Flows: Experiences in the Caribbean.* **Boulder, CO: Westview Press, 1991.**

When small countries become industrialized, many factors affect the economy. At first many new jobs may be created. Soon, however, exploitation of the working class and jobs lost to mechanization can cause an intensive emigration similar to that from the Caribbean in recent decades.

Palmer, Ransford W., ed. *In Search of a Better Life: Perspectives on Migration from the Caribbean.* **New York: Praeger, 1990.**

This collection of essays deals with the modern period of migration from the Caribbean, both to North America and to England. Discusses in detail the changes in economics that caused changes in the emigrating demographics.

Pastor, Robert A., ed. *Migration and Development in the Caribbean: The Unexplored Connection.* **Boulder, CO: Westview Press, 1985.**

As the Caribbean nations continue to have a difficult time with development, sizable portions of their populations emigrate to Great Britain, Canada, and the United States. This book explores the question of whether the loss of people hinders economic advancement in the Caribbean.

Sutton, Constance P., and Chaney, Elsa M. *Caribbean Life in New York City: Sociocultural Dimensions.* **New York: Center for Migration Studies, 1987.**

People have been coming to New York from the islands of the Caribbean Sea for decades. The various waves of immigrants have found welcome from those of their compatriots who came before them, and several distinct Caribbean communities are thriving in the city.

VIDEO

Goin' to Chicago. **Directed by George King, 1994. Distributed by California Newsreel, 149 Ninth Street, San Francisco, CA 94103.**

The migration of African Americans from the rural South to Chicago is traced through the personal stories of a group of elderly Chicagoans who left the Mississippi Delta.

Family Across the Sea. **Directed by Tim Carrier, 1991. Distributed by California Newsreel, 149 Ninth Street, San Francisco, CA 94103.**

This film traces the connection between the Gullah people of South Carolina's Sea Islands and the people of Sierra Leone. The film concludes with a Gullah group's emotional visit to Sierra Leone.

AFRICAN AMERICAN THEATER, FILM, AND TELEVISION

Black Film Review. Washington, DC: Domino Impressions.

> This quarterly journal is produced by the Black Film Institute of the University of the District of Columbia. It includes criticism and history, with contributions by students, directors, and scholars. Subscription information can be obtained from Sojourner Productions, 2025 I Street NW, Washington, DC 20001.

Bogle, Donald. *Blacks in American Films and TV*. New York: Garland, 1988.

> This is in the convenient format of an encyclopedia. Can't quite remember the name of that cop show that starred Bill Cosby in the 1960s? Look up his name, and get all his credits. On the other hand, you can look up *I Spy* if you forget Bill Cosby's name!

————.*Toms, Coons, Mulattoes, Mammies, and Bucks*. New York: Continuum 1994.

> The title lists the most common derogatory terms used through the 1940s by both the public and film industry professionals to describe African American film actors. These terms even appeared in film titles. The book is an appreciation of the performers who endured this constant racism to contribute to the form of film.

Cripps, Thomas. *Black Film as Genre*. Bloomington: Indiana University Press, 1978.

> The 1970s saw an explosion in movies made by African Americans. Cripps attempts to find common threads in the plots of the films and the storytelling techniques used by the directors to help define black film as a genre, or type, of moviemaking.

Fountain, Leatrice Gilbert. *Dark Star*. New York: St. Martin's Press, 1985.

In the early years of cinema, before Morgan Freeman and Denzel Washington were household names, many African Americans were involved in cinema and achieved various levels of star status. This book explores their careers, from that of Bill "Bojangles" Robinson, a world-renowned star with limited roles in white films, to Lorenzo Tucker, who was given romantic leads—but only in all-black films.

Gray, John. *Blacks in Film and Television*. Westport, CT: Greenwood Press, 1990.

This is a bibliography and filmography on African Americans' contributions to and comments on Hollywood and Television. It includes catalogs, encyclopedias, studies about various genres and stereotyping, histories of the industries, and biographies.

Hill, George; Raglin, Lorraine; and Johnson, Chas Floyd. *Black Women in Television*. New York: Garland, 1990.

Looking through this illustrated history and bibliography of black women's contribution to American TV, one is struck with how profound that contribution has been. Features include Lisa Bonet of *The Cosby Show*, Marla Gibbs of *The Jeffersons*, Charlayne Hunter-Gault of the *MacNeil/Lehrer News Hour*, and many others.

***History of Blacks in Film*. Los Angeles: William Grant Still Community Arts Center, 1983.**

This is the catalog of an exhibition that took place in Los Angeles in 1983. You'll see photos of African Americans involved in the movies, stills from the films themselves, and other artifacts that document the seventy-five-year history of blacks in film.

***A Pan-African Bibliography of Films, Filmmakers, and Performers*. Westport, CT: Greenwood Press, 1990.**

By "Pan-African," the editor means any country or region where the African cultural diaspora has had an effect on filmmaking. This concentrates on the United States, Caribbean, Latin America, and Britain.

Pfaff, Françoise. *Twenty-Five Black American Filmmakers*. Westport, CT: Greenwood Press, 1988.

Spike Lee is the only name that comes to mind when many people are asked to name a black filmmaker. John Singleton (*Boyz N the Hood*) has also gained recognition. But many people don't know that blacks have been making films in America since the late 1920s.

AFRICAN FILMS

Schipper, Mineke. *Theater and Society in Africa*. Athens: Ohio University Press, 1982.

Traditional African theater was a means of commenting on what was happening in and around the village, a way to release tensions, and to warn nonconforming community members to reconsider their actions. This book looks at African theater's power to reflect real life.

Ukadika, Nwachukwu Frank. *Black African Cinema*. Berkeley: University of California Press, 1994.

This film historian offers plots and statistics for important films made south of the Sahara. The book also gives profiles of important directors and includes historical background on filmmaking in Africa and the politics involved.

Wiley, David. *Africa on Film and Videotape*. East Lansing: African Studies Center, Michigan State University, 1982.

This catalog, complete with stats and plot summary for each picture, covers the years 1960–1980. It is a good place to start if you want to see film footage of a certain area of Africa, or a cinematic commentary on a certain political situation.

***Djeli*. Directed by Kramo-Lanciné Fadika, 1982.**

This social commentary by a Côte d'Ivoire filmmaker considers the survival of ancient African caste systems in contemporary African society. It tells the story of a member of the *griot* (storyteller) caste (*djeli* is the Malinke word for *griot*). This *griot* falls in love with a woman of noble lineage, whom he is forbidden to marry because of traditional taboos against mixing castes.

The Exile. Directed by Oumarou Ganda, 1980.

Ganda was an important director from Niger. The main part of the film is a reenaction of an African tale about a man who offers to give his head in exchange for the opportunity to marry a beautiful princess. He gets the princess and for years tries to avoid the executioner's sword. However, his people are plagued by drought and famine, which can be stopped only when he gives his life as promised. Ultimately, this tale is told as an analogy of the responsibilities of government officials in Africa.

Guelwaar. Directed by Ousman Sembene, 1993.

Sembene makes a poignant commentary on contemporary aspects of traditional life among the Wolof people of Senegal. The story tells how the body of a deceased member of a Christianized Wolof village is accidentally buried in the cemetery of a Muslim Wolof village. Modern European ideas of laws and arbitration are useless in this deeply spiritual crisis, and in the end only the traditional community elders can resolve the situation.

Jom. Directed by Ababacar Samb, 1981.

Jom is a word from the Wolof language. Senegalese director Samb attempts in this film to define the concept of *jom*, which has no direct equivalent in English. It is a combination of the greatest human virtues: respect, dignity, and courage. It is a basic moral ideal according to which every person tries to live his or her life. To the Wolof, the presence of *jom* in a person is more impressive and powerful than wealth.

AFRICAN AMERICAN FILMS

***The Black King*. Directed by B. Pollard, 1932.**

The makers of this black independent film were brutally honest with themselves. Rather than bash the white community, which they had the forum to do, they made a film about how ironic it is that there is a deep-rooted class system in black society, just as there is among whites.

***Boyz N the Hood*. Directed by John Singleton, 1991.**

Singleton crashed onto the scene with this powerhouse of a film, made when the director was in his early twenty years. Starring Larry Fishburne and Ice Cube, *Boyz N the Hood* is a revolutionary, honest look at urban African American youth, using Los Angeles as backdrop.

***Bronze Buckaroo*. Directed by R. C. Kann, 1939.**

The American West had plenty of black cowboys, no matter what you usually see in the movies. This independently produced Western, starring Herb Jeffries, gives an idea of the black communities (and conflicts) that developed among cattle rangers in the nineteenth century.

***The Defiant Ones*. Directed by Stanley Kramer, 1958.**

Tony Curtis and Sidney Poitier star in this allegorical representation of the necessity for the many races on earth to work together. The two portray escaped convicts—one white, one black—who are chained together. Although they hate each other, they find that they are interdependent and learn to cooperate and trust each other.

***Do the Right Thing*. Directed by Spike Lee, 1989.**

Although he made some fine films before this one (including *School Daze* and *She's Gotta Have It*), Spike Lee really hit the big time with this courageous parable of racial tensions between blacks and Italians in Lee's native neighborhood of Bedford-Stuyvesant in New York. Shot in a style akin to a theater stage, *Do the Right Thing* has an original look, a deeply African American feel. Great performances by Lee, Danny Aiello, Giancarlo Esposito, John Turturro, and others.

For Colored Girls Who Have Considered Suicide, When the Rainbow Is Enuf. Directed by Oz Scott, 1982.

Ntozake Shange wrote a heartrending book of poetry, a no-holds-barred look at the life of typical African American young women. This is a visualization of those poems, featuring Alfre Woodward, Crystal Lilly, and others.

Hollywood Shuffle. Directed by Robert Townsend, 1987.

A movie by blacks about blacks in the movies. Townsend, as actor, director, and producer of the film, takes a biting, humorous look at the limited opportunities for African Americans in Hollywood throughout its history. Townsend cowrote the movie with the help of Keenen Ivory Wayans, who later became famous for his production of the TV show *In Living Color*.

The Littlest Rebel. Directed by David Butler, 1935.

Bill "Bojangles" Robinson was severely criticized during his career for being willing to play butlers and chauffeurs who wait upon white movie stars. Robinson answered that at least he was becoming a famous black, and there were few enough of those. In the 1930s he was the highest paid movie star of all time, of any race. This is one of his classics, playing a companion to little Shirley Temple, whom he teaches to dance.

Native Son. Directed by Pierre Chenal, 1951.

Richard Wright wrote the novel upon which this film was based and also starred as the frustrated, intelligent Bigger Thomas. This was the first openly rebellious black movie made in Hollywood. Bigger cannot cope with the fact that bigotry alone bars him from his dreams, and his story ends in tragedy.

Tap! **Directed by Nick Castle, 1989.**

Gregory Hines stars in this celebration of jazz tap dancing. The plot is silly and incidental. Watch this for the great hoofing by masters such as Bunny Briggs, Steve Condos, "Sandman" Sims, and Sammy Davis, Jr. Also features young hot-shot Savion Glover.

Zydecko Mulatto. Directed by Jacob Munch, 1983.

African and Caribbean sounds swirl with European fiddling techniques in Zydeco music. This charming documentary focuses on a group of struggling, aspiring musicians in Filau-Fond, Louisiana. It touches on all aspects of Zydeco culture, including even some recipes and gardening tips.

AFRICAN MUSIC

Adé, King Sunny and the New African Beats.
Live at the Hollywood Palace. I.R.S., 1994.

Sunny and the Beats set Hollywood on fire with this white-hot 1990 live show. Adé's original compositions highlight his unmatched talent for making the thrilling traditions of African music breathe through a mix of ancient and modern instruments.

Africa Moves. Cambridge: Rounder, 1987.

Put on your dancing shoes and move those hips to the sounds of soukous, highlife, and juju music, some of the leading styles of current African pop. You will hear influences in every direction: ancient African sounds that have helped to shape reggae and rap, as well as a rock and roll beat that made its way to Africa from the United States.

Africa Never Stand Still. Ellipses Arts, 1994.

If you want a high-quality basic introduction to the modern side of African music, look no further than this impressive three-CD set. It presents a vast array of African pop and traditional artists, including Ladysmith Black Mambazo, Ali Farka Toure, and Youssou N'Dour. Comes with an informative and lavishly illustrated fifty-page booklet.

Ancient Ceremonies. Electra/Nonesuch, 1982.

The dance, instrumental music, and songs of traditional Ghana ethnic groups are celebrated on this CD. Joyous, frenzied dances call the spirit world to make itself known here on earth, while mesmerizing ballads tell thousands of years of history and pay respect to the ancestors.

Diagne, Boubacar. *Tabala Wolof.* **Village Pulse, 1994.**

This exciting CD features Sufi drumming from Senegal. The intricate beats are accompanied by chants and songs. This stuff makes your soul want to dance.

Maal, Baaba. *Firin' in Fourta.* **Mango, 1994.**

Maal has a poison tongue when he sings of the political situation in his native Senegal. He is especially biting about the problems left behind by the French. All sneering disappears from his voice, however, when he sings praises to the Muslim leaders of his community. The multi-talented musician sings in French, plays several instruments, and his sound never lacks for a dense forest of percussive rhythms.

N'Dour, Youssou. *Eyes Open.* **Columbia, 1992.**

N'Dour is one of the leaders in Senegalese music today. This hit album shows him at his powerful best, as he combines the pulsing rhythms of his ancient African past with political commentary on his country's current situation.

AFRICAN AMERICAN MUSIC

Anderson, Marian. *Tribute to Marian Anderson.* **ProArte, 1993.**

The unparalleled coloratura soprano voice of Marian Anderson (1902–1992) drove her singing career from her childhood to her retirement. She strove for greatness as a singer while quietly resisting and fighting extraordinary racial obstacles. She recorded a great deal of classical music, but has also recorded gospel music. Some of her gospel and Negro spirituals appear on this album.

Berry, Chuck. *The Chess Box*. Chess Music, 1994.

A big box set of one of the originators of rock music. You can hear the blues roots plainly in Berry's approach, even as he spearheads a new musical genre. This compilation features seventy-one recordings—200 minutes of material—that include previously unreleased tracks, versions, and mixes.

***Calypso from Trinidad*. Folklyric, 1992.**

An introduction to calypso as a powerful tool for satire and political comment. This music is the expression of rage at political intrigue and violence in the 1930s in Trinidad. Features Calypso greats Attila the Hun, Lord Executor, The Howler, and others.

Coltrane, John. *Africa/Brass and The Africa/Brass Sessions, Vol. II*. MCA Impulse, 1988.

John Coltrane spent a number of productive years playing with Dizzy Gillespie and Miles Davis before breaking off to lead his own groups in the late 1950s. On this double CD, "Trane" fuses his well-developed jazz feeling with explorations into the music of Africa.

Davis, Miles, with Sonny Fortune, Pete Cosey, Michael Henderson, et al. *Pangaea*. Columbia Jazz Contemporary Masters, 1990.

Recorded live at Osaka Festival Hall in 1975. Trumpeter Miles Davis's career spanned some four decades. His early years saw masterful contributions in the bebop and cool styles of jazz. This recording comes from his later career, in which he included East Indian and other influences to try to find a freer musical style.

*The Gospel Tradition: The Roots and the Branches,
Vol. 1.* **Columbia/Legacy, 1991.**

Bessie Smith, Blind Willie Johnson, Sister Myrtle Fields, and many other gospel singers and groups adorn this collection of gospel greats. The appearance here of Bessie Smith (see below) is an indication of the close connection between gospel and the blues.

Grandmaster Flash, Melle Mel, and the Furious Five.
*The Message from Beat Street: The Best of Grand-
master Flash, Melle Mel, and the Furious Five.*
Rhino Records, 1994.

This is a compilation of some of the earliest recorded rap. Flash and Melle Mel were members of the Furious Five in the early 1980s.

**Henderson, Fletcher, with Don Redmon, Louis
Armstrong, Coleman Hawkins, et al.** *Fletcher
Henderson and His Orchestra, 1924.* **Classics.**

Hear some of the jazz greats from the Harlem Renaissance on this record.

**Holiday, Billie, with Lester Young, Roy Eldridge,
Teddy Wilson, etc.** *The Quintessential Billie Holiday.*
Columbia, 1987–91.

A series of nine CDs documents the career of a great and tragic American singer. The recordings date from 1936 to 1940.

Jackson, Michael. *HIStory.* **Sony, 1995.**

A two-volume set including greatest hits and new material by "The King of Pop."

Joplin, Scott. *Treemonisha.* **Distributed by Sony Music
Video Enterprises, 1976.**

Scott Joplin (1868–1917) is mostly known for his composition of ragtime songs, but *Treemonisha* is the ragtime opera that occupied his efforts for much of his later life.

This posthumous performance of his composition is captured on video.

Leadbelly. *Lead Belly's Last Sessions*. **Smithsonian/ Folkways, 1994.**

Huddy Ledbetter, the great blues singer known around the world as Leadbelly, pulls out all the stops in these final sessions from the 1940s. Favorites include "Midnight Special," "Bluetail Fly," and "Easy Rider." Leadbelly showed up at one of these sessions without his guitar, so the listener is treated to unaccompanied traditional shouts and hollers.

Lion, Jah. *Columbia Colly*. **Island/UK, 1994.**

Lion is one of the lions of reggae. Here he is at the cutting edge, relying as much on the political satire in his lyrics as on weird, state-of-the-art studio mix tricks.

Marley, Bob, and the Wailers. *Legend*. **Tuff Gong/ Island, 1990.**

From Jamaica came musicians and an art form that have influenced people the world over. In the 1960s and '70s, Bob Marley and his band the Wailers took the world by storm with their mastery of reggae music and their understanding of its musical, social, and political possibilities. Hear their greatest hits on this classic album.

McBride, Christian, with Joshua Redman, Cyrus Chestnut, Steve Turre, Lewis Nash, et al. *Gettin' to It*. **Verve, 1995.**

This brand-new album features several of the bright new faces in modern jazz. Bass player McBride and his bandmates are making sure that jazz will still be thriving well into the twenty-first century.

Morton, Jelly Roll, with the Red Hot Peppers, King Oliver, Voltaire de Faut, et al. *The Pianist and Composer*. **Smithsonian, 1991–92.**

New Orleans' Ferdinand Joseph la Menthe, known to the world as Jelly Roll Morton, was a giant of jazz in the 1920s. His own multiethnic (African and European) roots somehow symbolize the mix of African and European elements that are found in jazz. These three CDs are a fine introduction to the early master.

Parker, Charlie, with Dizzy Gillespie, Red Rodney, and John Lewis. *Bird at Carnegie Hall.* **Cool n' Blue, 1992.**

These recordings were made from various concerts between 1947 and 1954. Alto saxophonist Charlie Parker, known as "Bird," is still revered by many as the greatest jazzman of all time. He and Dizzy Gillespie were at the forefront of the innovative bebop movement in jazz during the 1940s. Many musicians who played in his bands, including Charles Mingus and Miles Davis, went on to lead bands on their own. Parker died in 1955 at the age of thirty-four.

Parker, Charlie, and Gillespie Dizzy, with Thelonious Monk, Curley Russell, and Buddy Rich. *Bird and Diz.* **Verve, 1950.**

In the 1980s, trumpeter Dizzy Gillespie made an appearance on *The Cosby Show*, where he showed off his wildly inflatable cheeks to roars of studio audience applause. Although his cheeks helped bring him musical fame, he was also known as a humorous, warmhearted person. He appears here with Parker and pianist Thelonious Sphere Monk, an astounding harmonic innovator. Drummer Buddy Rich's influence is so wide that a collection of jazz and rock and heavy metal drummers recently compiled a tribute album dedicated to him.

***Rapso.* (Various Artists) Kisskidee Rapso, 1994.**

Rapso is a new African-rooted sound from Trinidad. Its many influences include soca, dub, ragga, rap, and calypso. Brother Resistance, one of the form's founders, is featured here, along with Home Front, Boyz N the Road, and others.

Smith, Bessie. *Empress of the Blues: The Complete Recordings.* **Columbia/Legacy.**

These four CDs appeared between 1991 and 1993 and document the storied career of the foremost blues singer of the 1920s.

Vaughan, Sarah, with Cannonball Adderley, Roy Haynes, Freddy Hubbard, Thad Jones, et al. *The Complete Sarah Vaughan on Mercury.* **Mercury, 1987.**

Spanning the years from 1954 to 1969, these four CDs chronicle the career of one of the finest singers in jazz. Swinging her way through standards, scatting her way through some tunes written especially for her, Vaughan teams up in these recordings with some great session musicians.

Vodu 155. *Vodu 155.* **Island Records, 1994.**

This group is from Brooklyn, but its sound celebrates the members' roots in Haiti. They've been described as "voodoo music with a hip-hop mentality," although even that is an oversimplification of their very original identity. Good mixing interweaves a pulsing Haitian ceremonial drum through many tracks.

Wilson, Cassandra, with Jean-Paul Bourelly, Kevin Bruce Harris, Kevin Johnson, et al. *Dance to the Drums Again.* **DIW/Columbia, 1993.**

In this and her other albums, Wilson receives inspiration from African musics ranging from West African traditional, to country blues, R & B, and classic jazz. But make no mistake: she infuses old and new with her own distinctive style.

AFRICAN DANCE

African Art and Motion. **Washington, DC: U.S. National Gallery of Art, 1974.**

This stunning collection of photographs of items in the National Gallery's holdings illustrate the connection between movement and beauty in the West African imagination. Traditional dance forms of many peoples are enhanced by these colorful, symbolic costumes and props.

Cole, Herbert, ed. *I Am Not Myself: The Art of African Masquerade*. Los Angeles: Museum of Cultural History, UCLA, 1985.

The gifted photographer Herbert Cole traveled in the Sahel and sub-Saharan Africa to record the amazing colors, imagery, and diversity of traditional mask-dancing. From the Dogon masked stilt-walkers to Hausa rattan-covered masked medicine men, there is no end of fascination in these photos.

Darbois, Dominique. *African Dance: A Book of Photographs*. Prague: Artia, 1962.

Many peoples are celebrated in this portrait of the dance traditions of Africa south of the Sahara. From stilt dancing among the Dogon to the rustling rattan costumes of the Hausa, this provides a good overview of many cultures. The text by V. Vasut explains the ritual significance of the dances and tries to find a common thread among them.

***Queen of Angels*. Produced by KCET-TV, Los Angeles, 1981.**

The R'wanda Lewis Dance Company is featured in this hour-long video. Her troupe traces the influence of African and Afro-Caribbean dances on the development of African American movement. Includes the piece "Homeland Africa," taking its steps from West African ceremony, as well as American dance forms such as the Cakewalk and the Charleston.

Warren, Lee. *The Dance of Africa: An Introduction*. Englewood Cliffs, NJ: Prentice-Hall, 1972.

Meant for a young audience, this is a fun book on basic

African dance moves. It includes instructions for doing the dances, as well as photos of each movement.

AFRICAN AMERICAN DANCE

Dancing: New World, New Forms. **Produced by Rhoda Grauer, 1993.**

This is a fascinating video series about dance styles developed in the Americas after the influence of nonindigenous populations. Volume five explores how African dance traditions have developed in the Americas. It includes South American capoeira, African American tap, and the fascinating black fraternity step dancing.

Emery, Lynne Fauley. *Black Dance in the United States from 1619 to 1970.* **New York: Dance Horizons, 1980.**

Emery's important work starts with the year the first British slaving ship landed in the American colonies. It traces African-influenced dance forms from plantation ringshouts to the Alvin Ailey Company.

Frank, Rusty E. *Tap! The Greatest Tap Dance Stars and Their Stories, 1900–1955.* **New York: William Morrow, 1991.**

Although it does not exclusively feature black dancers, this lovely photo-essay book does give an impression of the extent to which black American tap influenced the dancing of both black and white stars of stage and screen.

Lerma, Dominique-Rene de. *Black Music in Our Culture.* **Kent, OH: Kent State University Press, 1970.**

If you have ever danced hip-hop or even disco, you might want to think about why those moves are the way they are. They are hugely indebted to the rhythms and harmonies present in the music that accompanies them. That special electrifying beat came to America through African and Caribbean slaves, whose descendants developed blues, jazz, and rock 'n' roll.

Portrait of Carmencita Romero. **Produced by Black Arts, Atlanta, 1983.**

> Romero was one of the finest dancers to work with Katherine Dunham. This fifty-six-minute video shows her strong roots in Afro-Caribbean dance, as well as her original contributions to the form. Especially interesting for its long sequence in the classroom.

Rethinking the Balanchine Legacy. **Produced by the Jerome Robbins Archive, 1993.**

> This is a huge project, spanning 339 minutes of tape. George Balanchine is possibly the most famous and most influential choreographer of this century. The idea behind the series is to examine just what his influences were. Traditional Afro-Caribbean as well as black American jazz dance forms are very important to his work.

Southern, Eileen, and Wright, Josephine. *African American Traditions in Song, Sermon, Tale and Dance, 1600s–1920.* **Westport, CT: Greenwood, 1990.**

> The editors have put together a huge, annotated bibliography leading to sources on the African oral and movement arts. The years covered span the most intensive period of slave trading to the early days of the glorious Harlem Renaissance.

Stearns, Jean, and Stearns, Marshall. *Jazz Dance, The Story of American Vernacular Dance.* **New York: Da Capo, 1994 (first printed 1968).**

> It was a tragedy for people interested in dance when this book went out of print. Thanks to requests from the dance community, Da Capo has brought it back. Thorough consideration is given to the African roots of American dance forms, the exact contributions of particular dancers, along with lots of photos.

That's Black Entertainment. **Produced by VCI Inc., 1989.**

This hour-long video is a celebration of music and dance by blacks in film. From the taps of Bill Robinson and Sammy Davis, Jr., to the Afro-modern moves from the movie *Fame*, these are joyous reminders of the African American dance tradition.

Thorpe, Edward. *Black Dance*. London: Chatto & Windus, 1989.

Thorpe traces African American dance movements and rhythms as far back in Africa as possible, trying to tie particular steps with particular peoples and regions in Africa. He covers not only vernacular jazz and rhythm tap, but also African-influenced classical dance, as exemplified by such choreographers as Alvin Ailey.

Wright, Arthur. *Color Me White*. Smithtown, NY: Exposition Press, 1980.

Arthur Wright was an African American dancer in vaudeville who had a very unusual thing happen to his career. Because of a rare pigmentation disorder, his dark skin turned white! In this autobiography he describes how this bizarre circumstance affected how others saw him and how he saw himself.

An African American Photo Album

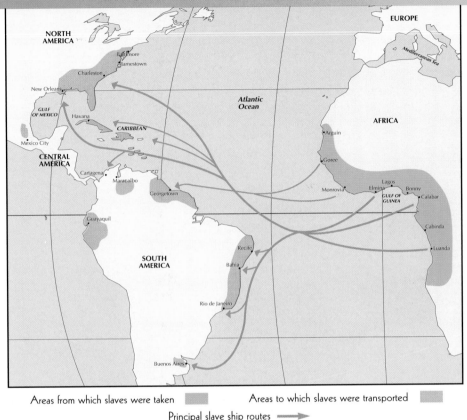

Areas from which slaves were taken ▢   Areas to which slaves were transported ▢

Principal slave ship routes ➡

The United States has been called a nation of immigrants. In most cases those immigrants came to this country voluntarily. The case of Africans, however, was quite different. The ancestors of most African Americans were brought to the Americas by force—victims of an economic system of exploitation and brutality known as slavery. The slave trade treated Africans as cargo to be bought and sold, shipped and traded. Even the abolition of slavery by constitutional amendment in 1865 did not yet bring freedom. Injustice, racism, violence, and hatred continued to plague the lives of African Americans. They were forced to fight for every freedom and for equality with white Americans in the workplace, in schools, on public transportation, and in virtually every other area of their lives. That fight continues today.

In the face of tremendous adversity, African Americans sought to preserve elements of their African heritage while at the same time forging a new African diaspora culture. It is characterized by musical and dance forms, religious practices, art and architecture, handicrafts, foods, language, and many other elements that in turn have influenced and enriched the culture of all Americans.

The Yoruba live in Nigeria on the Atlantic Coast, which was the site of the majority of slave trading between Africans and Europeans. It is estimated that 1.5 million Yoruba people were sold into slavery. They sustained much of their culture in the Americas and profoundly influenced the development of culture there.

The Asante continue the traditional practice of drumming. In the Americas, most slave owners, fearing that slaves would be able to communicate with each other in this way, outlawed drumming and blowing of horns.

Kwanzaa is a uniquely African American celebration that takes place in late December and early January. A seven-day festival, its observance was begun in 1966 by M. Ron Karenga, an African American activist. Karenga modeled Kwanzaa after a traditional African harvest festival. His goal was to increase African Americans' awareness of their African heritage and celebrate qualities such as unity, self-determination, and cooperation in the African American community.

Above, a family listens to a Kwanzaa reading.

A woman lights candles at a pre-Kwanzaa ceremony at a church in New York City.
The Kwanzaa celebration involves the exchange of gifts and an African-inspired meal called karamu.

Young members of the Le Rocque Bey dance troupe participate in the African American Day Parade in Harlem, in New York City.

Children in Philadelphia explore the traditional African art of drumming at an African American cultural celebration called Odunde.

Frequently it happened that a slave was sold initially in the Caribbean and then transported to the United States. Slave traders believed that this would help the Africans adjust to "civilized" culture. In the West Indies Africans developed a richly distinct culture; this culture has found its way to the United States with more recent immigrants from countries such as Jamaica, Trinidad, Haiti, and the Dominican Republic. Above, a young girl in an elaborate costume participates in the West Indian Festival in Brooklyn, New York.

Young women in festive clothing participate in a Caribbean Day Parade.

In Tucson, Arizona, participants in a Martin Luther King, Jr. Day March wear the uniforms of the "buffalo soldiers," which is what Native Americans called the African American soldiers who fought in the U.S. Cavalry in the 1870s.

Interest in African and African American history has increased in recent years. An African American girl explores the books displayed at an African American "read-in."

African Americans participate in the sixth annual Tribute to the Ancestors at Sea in Coney Island,
New York. The ceremony commemorates those Africans who died on their way to the Americas
during the transatlantic crossing known as the Middle Passage.

The Tribute to the Ancestors at Sea originated in the Caribbean, but has more recently begun to be celebrated by African Americans in the United States.

African Americans have struggled against barriers of racism and discrimination while seeking to achieve their full potential as members of American society. Hiram Revels, the first African American lawyer to argue a case before the United States Supreme Court, is depicted in this 1880 woodcut.

Ernest G. Deveaux, Jr., a member of the first African American police squad in Charleston, South Carolina, holds a 1952 photo of the squad.

Alice Walker's novels are evocative of the African and African American experience. *The Color Purple* depicted the life of an African American woman in the first half of this century who maintained her dignity and vision against tremendous odds. It was made into a film by Steven Spielberg and launched the career of Oprah Winfrey.

Chapter 4
Getting Started on Your Search

Talking to Your Relatives

It is one thing to know the history of blacks in the United States. It is quite different to learn how your own ancestors were involved in that history. That's what family research teaches—your kin's personal experiences in and contributions to the development of America.

There will be plenty of opportunities in your search to dig through large books and scan microfiche for information on ancestors long dead. The key to getting a flying start on a family history search is to begin with the living. The personal memories and stories you gain from talking to your relatives are just as valuable as any facts you'll find.

Ask everyone in your household to help you make a list of all the relatives they can think of. You probably won't be able to come up with all your living relations; over time, however, new names will surface. You can always interview new-found kin later in the process.

Start by interviewing yourself. Jot answers to some questions into a notebook, or talk into a tape recorder. Tell your name, birthdate, place of birth; the dates and locations of any religious rituals you've participated in (such as baptism); all the different places you've lived, along with the street address in each town (if you remember) and the schools you've attended.

Then make a record of whatever bits of the family's oral history you recall. These could be events that you lived through or witnessed, such as your grandfather's funeral or the birth of your niece. Or they could be legends that other people have told you about family members. These are the kinds of stories that you should encourage your relatives to tell. Even if they've been exaggerated over the years, they all still have a kernel of truth that can be an invaluable clue.

Ask your parents for their vital statistics: place and date of birth, religious rituals, place and date of marriage. Have them give you whatever information they know about their parents. Your mom or dad may be able to fill in details that you missed when you interviewed yourself. They will also remember events from long before you were born. Ask them where and when they lived and moved, both as adults and kids. Get their versions of some family legends.

To get similar information from your other relatives, it is usually best to send a polite letter explaining that you are doing research on the family and would be grateful if they would share their valuable memories with you. You might send a stamped, self-addressed envelope and a list of questions, such as:

- Who is the earliest ancestor you know about? Approximately where and when did he or she live?
- Give the following statistics about yourself, your spouse, and your children: name; place and date of birth, place and date of marriages, deaths, and burials; where you have lived and when.
- Give as many of the above facts as you can for your parents and grandparents.
- Do you have any personal or legal papers or any photographs relating to your family?
- Do you know of any partial family history already researched or written by any of our relatives?

It's great if you get back a lot of filled-in surveys like these. Even better, though, is the chance to interview the relatives in person. Not all of them will be willing, and some will live too far away to visit. Telephone interviews are possible, but it's especially hard to get a person you don't know well to open up to you over the phone.

If you get a chance to interview some relatives in person,

be sure to ask permission to tape-record—or even videotape—your chat. Come to the interview prepared with questions, but also give your relative a chance to wander off the subject.

In African American genealogical research, a terribly difficult subject that you will eventually need to broach with the elders of your family is slavery. As we near the twenty-first century it becomes less and less likely that you will meet relatives who even have personal recollections of ancestors who were slaves, but they may have memories of their elders talking about slavery. This pain-healing distance is good for genealogists because it means more people will be willing to talk about their family's involvement in slavery.

After you have completed an interview, type a transcript of it and send it to the relative, along with a note of thanks for the valuable cooperation.

Organizing Your Search

As you talk to relatives or receive their questionnaires, you will begin to compile a list of names, places, events, and dates having to do with members of your family. Before that pile of information becomes overwhelming, it's time to set up a nice, simple way to record facts and store documents.

Every genealogist has a slightly different style of organizing. All that matters is that it be consistent and simple enough to allow you to find what you need when you need it. In any case, it's good to start with a three-ring binder and looseleaf paper for taking notes, a bunch of file folders for organizing your notes, and a box to keep the files in.

The time-honored method of keeping track of information on your ancestors is by using two forms: family group sheets and pedigree charts (see illustrations on pages 95–96). Both of these forms are available for photocopying at any library with a genealogy department. Inquire at the reference desk.

A family group sheet records each nuclear family unit: a couple and their children. Under each name on the sheet you record the person's place and date of birth, the parent's place and date of marriage, and any death dates. If either of the parents had another marriage, he or she is given a separate family group sheet for that marriage and its offspring. Use the file folders to hold the family group sheets, one per folder, along with any documents you find pertaining to that nuclear family.

The pedigree chart is a linear history of all of these family groups, from you back to your earliest known ancestor. Carry a copy of the pedigree chart with you whenever you go to do research. It gives you an at-a-glance picture of just what facts you're still missing. It's also a good idea to send a copy of your pedigree chart to all of the relatives you contact.

One way to spare yourself a lot of frustration is to realize right off the bat that you're not going to complete your pedigree chart. Only experienced genealogists who can devote decades of time (and considerable money) to the project can do a thorough history reaching back several centuries. The probability of that much success is even less for people of African American heritage, because there are so few records on blacks before the late nineteenth century.

Instead of tackling everything at once and setting yourself up for disappointment, it's best to go gradually. Choose one surname, and take it back three or four generations until things get sticky. Then, instead of staying in a maddening rut, come back to the present and try another family line.

Where do you find the information to fill in your family group sheets and pedigree charts? Contrary to what you might expect, you can't just ask your relatives. In genealogy a strict distinction is made between information from hearsay and information from an official paper. The first kind can be called oral tradition, although it can also include letters and diaries that describe something secondhand (Cousin Joe writes to tell Aunt Mary that Cousin Sue had a baby on May 3, 1949). The second kind is called documented evidence. No matter how reliable your source, information received through oral tradition is not considered a fact until it has been backed up by documented evidence.

Vital records are the most important kind of documented

Pedigree Chart

Name of Compiler _____

Address _____

City, State _____

Date _____

Person No.1 on this chart is the same person as No.____ on chart No.____.

Chart No.____

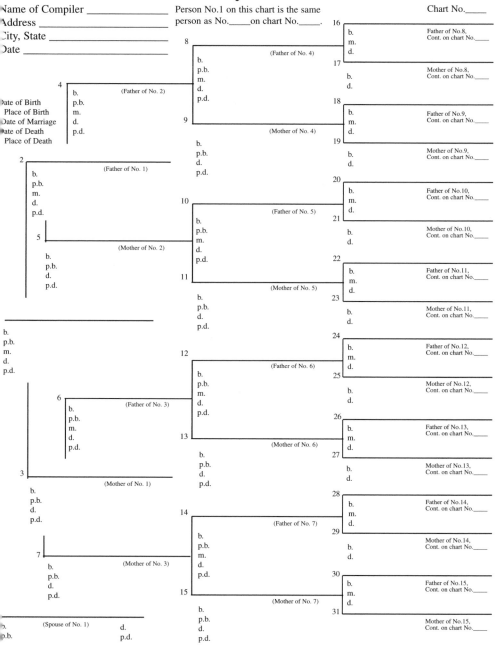

4 (Father of No. 2)
b.
p.b.
m.
d.
p.d.

2 (Father of No. 1)
b.
p.b.
m.
d.
p.d.

5 (Mother of No. 2)
b.
p.b.
d.
p.d.

Date of Birth
Place of Birth
Date of Marriage
Date of Death
Place of Death

b.
p.b.
m.
d.
p.d.

6 (Father of No. 3)
b.
p.b.
m.
d.
p.d.

3 (Mother of No. 1)
b.
p.b.
d.
p.d.

7 (Mother of No. 3)
b.
p.b.
d.
p.d.

8 (Father of No. 4)
b.
p.b.
m.
d.
p.d.

9 (Mother of No. 4)
b.
p.b.
d.
p.d.

10 (Father of No. 5)
b.
p.b.
m.
d.
p.d.

11 (Mother of No. 5)
b.
p.b.
d.
p.d.

12 (Father of No. 6)
b.
p.b.
m.
d.
p.d.

13 (Mother of No. 6)
b.
p.b.
d.
p.d.

14 (Father of No. 7)
b.
p.b.
m.
d.
p.d.

15 (Mother of No. 7)
b.
p.b.
d.
p.d.

16 Father of No.8, Cont. on chart No.____
b.
m.
d.

17 Mother of No.8, Cont. on chart No.____
b.
d.

18 Father of No.9, Cont. on chart No.____
b.
m.
d.

19 Mother of No.9, Cont. on chart No.____
b.
d.

20 Father of No.10, Cont. on chart No.____
b.
m.
d.

21 Mother of No.10, Cont. on chart No.____
b.
d.

22 Father of No.11, Cont. on chart No.____
b.
m.
d.

23 Mother of No.11, Cont. on chart No.____
b.
d.

24 Father of No.12, Cont. on chart No.____
b.
m.
d.

25 Mother of No.12, Cont. on chart No.____
b.
d.

26 Father of No.13, Cont. on chart No.____
b.
m.
d.

27 Mother of No.13, Cont. on chart No.____
b.
d.

28 Father of No.14, Cont. on chart No.____
b.
m.
d.

29 Mother of No.14, Cont. on chart No.____
b.
d.

30 Father of No.15, Cont. on chart No.____
b.
m.
d.

31 Mother of No.15, Cont. on chart No.____
b.
d.

(Spouse of No. 1)
b.
p.b.
d.
p.d.

FAMILY GROUP WORK SHEET #_____

HUSBAND, Name:

Birth: Place:
Death: Place:
Burial: Place:
Father:
Mother:
Occupation:
Notes:

WIFE, Name:

Birth: Place:
Death: Place:
Burial: Place:
Father:
Mother:
Occupation:
Notes:

Name	Date & Place of Birth	Marriage	Date & Place of Death	Married to	Date & Place of Birth Death

evidence. If you found the letter described above, you still need to find the birth certificate for Sue's baby to prove its birthdate and birthplace. For that matter, you need the birth and marriage certificates of both Joe and Sue in order to complete their records. Aunt Mary passed away in 1970, so you will need her death certificate and burial registration in addition to her other vital records.

Wills, tax returns, military papers, school report-cards and

Military records can be useful in finding information on a relative who served in the armed forces. Many African Americans served with distinction, such as these Navy steward mates who received Bronze Stars for their courage and skill when fighting in the Pacific theater during World War II.

diplomas, medical records, bank statements, passports, and employment contracts are other examples of documents that are considered "fact" in genealogy.

The first place to look for official documents is in your relatives' houses. There is no end to what might be stored in a grandmother's attic. Promise to handle everything with care, and she may let you look through an old box containing all sorts of useful stuff. Ask whether you can borrow these things, at least long enough to have them photocopied. Be sure to write on the back of each photocopy exactly where you found the document.

You won't find every vital record you'd like in the possession of your relatives. Fortunately, there are other places to get them. Write to the addresses listed in the **Resources** section of this chapter to find out how to order records that you can't find.

Birth certificates and income tax returns don't make up a quarter of the treasures you may find among your relatives' things. Keep an eye out for diaries, letters, and photographs. Listen if your host tries to tell you about some object. If he's holding up a rag doll and saying, "Gramps got this when his troops were stationed in Vienna," don't sit there wondering what you're going to do with an old ragdoll. Think, "Hey! His grandfather was in the military in Vienna!" That's a great clue.

While you're looking through your ancestors' property, take the opportunity to let your imagination wander. Ask about things, and you'll hear amazing stories that will make your past come to life. That old, beat-up piano was kept in the family because someone saved six months' wages to buy it and was the first African American in his town to have one. That quilt was made by female ancestors in Georgia, probably around 1850. The time and place make it very likely that they were slaves. Can you see anger or sorrow in their art? Or were they so full of love for the baby they wrapped in it that no earthly indignities could dampen their spirits?

Graveyards

If you can travel to some of the places where your ancestors lived, it is worthwhile to search for their gravesites in area cemeteries. You may know what religion a relative professed and be able to get help finding his grave from the local chapter of that denomination. Or see if there is an index to historic gravesites published for that county.

Gravestones can take the place of a missing burial certificate. You need to take a photograph or a rubbing of the stone. Rubbings are actually better, because you can see what you're getting as you work. It takes some experience to get a photo of a tombstone that shows the lettering legibly. Some very old stones have been eroded by rain and pollution.

Besides the ancestor's name and dates, tombstones sometimes mention the names of a spouse, child, or parents.

They also sometimes contain epitaphs. The verses memorializing ancestors from the slavery era can be especially moving:

God wills us Free, Man wills us Slaves.
I will as God wills, God's will be done.

Though born in a land of slavery [Africa]
He was born free.
Though he lived in a land of liberty,
He lived a slave.

—from *Black Genealogy* by Charles L. Blockson and Ron Fry (see **Resources**).

Working in the Library

Not all of a genealogist's work can take place in a hands-on environment. A great deal of the information you need must be dug up from indexes and record books at research libraries and historical archives.

Every state in America has several state archives, plus special collections at the county and local levels. To find these collections, write to the county courthouse in the area where your ancestor lived and inquire about how to find certain records. There are also public and private research libraries whose holdings include family and local history books, articles, and maps.

If you are unable to travel to all the counties from which you need information, you may be able to have the staff at certain facilities find some of the documents you're looking for. You will be required to fill out forms asking for specifics about the subject of the search, and there may be a fee for finding and photocopying documents.

Just like interviewing relatives, it's always best to do research in person. When you go to a genealogy library, ask a reference librarian how to find out whether there is a family history already published about the surname you're researching. There are indexes for published family histories, as well as resources that list a small percentage of unpublished genealogy manuscripts. You may get lucky.

It can be a little exasperating for an African American to find a book on the right surname, but the family turns out to be the wrong color. It's entirely possible that your ancestor chose this surname because he knew someone in that book. If you have the time, you could page through and see if these people were slave owners or perhaps helped freed slaves in some way. If you come up empty, don't despair. Make a note of the book's title, author, and call number, in case you want to go back to it later, and try something else.

No matter what you look at in a library, you should follow certain procedures that will make things a lot clearer when you look at your notes again at home. First, date each page, and note what library you took the notes in (you might want to devise an abbreviation for each place you visit). Make a complete notation of the book's author, title, publisher, publication date, and call number. Each time you take a piece of information from that book, indicate the page you found it on. If you make a photocopy from the book, jot down on the back which book it came from. Also make a note of whether you think this book might come in handy again later on (and why), or if it was completely useless.

Every genealogy library and most large public libraries have subscriptions to some of the family history magazines on the market. Inquire about these. Besides featuring articles on particular genealogical problems (you might find articles about doing African American research, for example), they have many classified advertisements. Genealogists rent space to advertise upcoming family reunions and to request information about certain surnames. It can be very rewarding to answer and place ads in such publications. Genealogists in general are eager to share information and like to hear from fellow family history fans. You will also find advertisements for national genealogy societies in these magazines (listed in the **Resources** sections of this book). It is always worthwhile to write to societies that look promising, to inquire about membership fees and privileges.

If there is a particular book that you can't find in the

library where you're working, ask a reference librarian whether it can be borrowed through interlibrary loan. This program allows libraries to borrow books from other library systems and archives.

You can find out for yourself where certain books are available by using the On-line Catalog of the Library of Congress. OCLC is available through the Internet, which you may be able to access at your school, home, or research library. It lists practically every book published in the United States and the library systems that own it. Once found, the book you need can then be ordered if the library that has it participates in interlibrary loan. Some materials are too fragile or rare to be shipped across the country, so they will not be available through this program. However, it can help you get at a lot of great resources.

Resources

SEARCHING IN THE UNITED STATES: MANUALS, BIBLIOGRAPHIES

American Genealogy: A Basic Course. **National Genealogical Society.**

> Write to NGS at 4527 17th Street North, Arlington, VA 22207-2363 for a brochure about this home-study program. It includes written and video material and is a great way to learn about organization and research skills before you hit the libraries.

Banaka, William H. *Training in Depth Interviewing*. New York: Harper & Row, 1971.

> Skilled interviewing isn't just a matter of sitting down and chatting. This book will give you tips for preparing, staying focused, and getting good answers from the interviewee.

Blockson, Charles L., and Fry, Ron. *Black Genealogy*. Englewood Cliffs, NJ: Prentice-Hall, 1977.

> One of the best and most complete manuals for tracing African American roots. Blockson treats every aspect of the search, with reproductions of indexes and registers you will encounter. He even treats the steps back to Africa, although he warns that a family historian's success at it is mostly based on luck.

Board for Certification of Genealogists P.O. Box 5816, Falmouth, VA 22403-5816.

> Send a self-addressed, stamped envelope and three dollars for a current list of certified family history researchers.

Colored Paths in Missouri. **Wright City, MO:
Wesley-Smith United Methodist Church, 1992.**

This church has done community research to help with
the accurate identification and documentation of information on African slaves and their descendants. It includes
cemetery evidence, oral history, census reports, and photos of blacks in Warren County, Missouri.

Directory of Professional Genealogists. **Salt Lake City,
UT: Association of Professional Genealogists, 1994.**

Look here for people who do advanced-level research in
genealogy. They charge by the hour, page, or project. The
index lists areas of specialty.

Dollarhide, William. *Managing a Genealogical
Project: A Complete Manual for the Management and
Organization of Genealogical Materials.* **Baltimore:
Genealogical Publishing, 1988.**

Common sense and lots of labeled folders are sometimes
not enough to keep a novice family researcher organized.
Take advantage of Dollarhide's vast experience; he's responsible for designing the best computer software for
genealogy organization, too.

**Evelyn Spears Family Group Sheet Exchange
East 12502 Frideger
Elk, WA 99009**

A service that provides previously researched family group
sheets for the requested surname. About ten dollars per
surname, with a catalog of 14,000 surnames.

Family History

This fifty-one-episode made-for-cable TV show empha-
sizes the fun and adventure of genealogical research while
giving practical advice. Each episode focuses on a particular aspect of genealogy, including particular heritage
searches, using archives and censuses, and computer software for family research. Available on videotape from:

Stephen Conte
P.O. Box 962
West Caldwell, NJ 07007

Genealogical Center, Inc.
International Family Group Sheet Exchange
P.O. Box 17698
Tampa, FL 33682

This service charges thirty cent per page, and each completed surname study is anywhere from 10 to 300 pages long. Write for catalog of 8,000 surnames.

Greenwood, Val D. *The Researcher's Guide to American Genealogy*. Baltimore: Genealogical Publishing, 1990.

Professional genealogists recommend this book as an excellent starting point that can lead you into an intermediate level of research and then guide you toward more advanced resources.

***A Handy Book for Genealogists*. Logan, UT: Everton Publishers, 1989.**

Everton is one of the major publishers of genealogical books and magazines for Americans. This is a good start-up guide from the pros.

***Heritage Quest*. American Genealogical Lending Library.**

The AGLL publishes this bimonthly magazine. In addition to the usual classified ads offering or seeking information and services, *Heritage Quest* features columns on computer technology and adoption searches. Write to: AGLL, 593 West North Street, Bountiful, UT 84011.

Schreiner-Yantis, Netti. *Genealogical and Local History Books in Print*, 3 vols. 4th ed. Springfield, VA, 1990.

This catalogs some rare manuscripts related to family research, a great resource to help you find out whether there are any books already available on your surname. It also lists vendors in the United States who sell various publications, supplies, and services of use to the genealogist.

Scott, Jean Sampson. *Beginning an Afro-American Genealogical Pursuit*. New York: Eppress Printers, 1985.

This is a very brief introduction to black genealogy. It gives an overview of the most important sources, where to find them, and the most common problems and stumbling blocks.

Smith, Gloria L. *Black Americana at Mount Vernon: Genealogy Techniques for Slave Group Research*. Tucson: G. L. Smith, 1984.

Using the example of George Washington's Virginia household, Smith illustrates some methods for the extremely difficult task of tracing African-American families through slavery.

Smith, Jessie Carney, ed. *Ethnic Genealogy: A Research Guide*. Westport, CT: Greenwood Press, 1983.

This book on tracing roots is for all American people of color: blacks, Asians, Hispanics, Native Americans. All these ethnicities have in common the fact that their past is not as well recorded in documents as that of European-Americans. It features a foreword by Alex Haley, author of *Roots*.

Stano, Michael E., and Reinsch, Jr., N. L. *Communication in Interviews*. Englewood Cliffs, NJ: Prentice-Hall, 1982.

These communication arts experts offer advice on interviewing that can be applied to family history chats with your relatives. They discuss ways to prepare before your talk, how to communicate your questions clearly, and how to read important signals (for example, if your relative is trying to tell you that a certain subject is uncomfortable to talk about).

Wasserman, P., and Kennington, A., eds. *Ethnic Information Sources of the United States.* **Detroit: Gale Research Co., 1983.**

An amazing sourcebook listing fraternities, cultural and educational organizations, heritage institutes, plus information on libraries and archives around the country and the strengths of their specific collections.

Wright, Norman, E. *Preserving Your American Heritage.* **Provo, UT: Brigham Young University Press, 1981.**

An inspiring book to send you on your way toward becoming a genealogist. Get a sense of the richness of the heritage quilt that makes up the United States. Includes useful information on genealogy procedure and sources, telling you how as well as why to trace your roots.

SOCIETIES AND JOURNALS

Afro-American Historical and Genealogical Society, Inc.
P.O. Box 73086
Washington, DC 20056-3086

It's a good idea to write to this association early in your search. You will receive information on membership as well as a list of their publications. They publish a journal and a newsletter, which are available in research libraries.

American Genealogical Lending Library
593 West North Street
P.O. Box 329
Bountiful, UT 84011

You can rent microforms of indexes (vital records, censuses, etc.) from AGLL for reasonable fees. They also offer transcripts of wills and deeds. Ask the staff of your local library whether they participate in AGLL rental programs.

Little by little, these indexes are also coming out on CD-ROM, and are for sale.

Association for State and Local History
172 Second Avenue North, Suite 102
Nashville, TN 37201

Write for a list of publications, and check a research library for a copy of their *Directory of Historical Organizations in the United States and Canada.* This is not specifically for genealogists, but the two subjects overlap considerably.

Meyer, Mary K. *Meyer's Directory of Genealogical Societies in the USA and Canada.* Mt. Airy, MD: Mary K. Meyer, 1988.

Check this book in a genealogical library to find out which societies have activities in your region, focus on your family's ethnic group and settlement area, publish useful catalogs and manuals, and have reasonable membership fees.

National Genealogical Society
4527 17th Street North
Arlington, VA 22207-2363

The NGS offers information and contacts for all ethnicities in America. One of the biggest American family research associations, the NGS publishes and sells books, forms, and indexes. Membership entitles you to the *National Genealogical Society Quarterly* and *NGS Newsletter,* which are also available in research libraries.

National Institute on Genealogical Research
P.O. Box 14274
Washington, DC 20044-4274

Write to inquire about this organization's publications and workshops.

Patriotic Societies
These organizations exist to serve American descendants of soldiers and statesmen and act as custodians of records. In-

cluded in their records are regimental information for "colored troops" from the Revolutionary War.

National Society
Daughters of the American Revolution
1776 D Street NW
Washington, DC 20006

National Society
Sons of the American Revolution
2412 Massachusetts Avenue
Washington, DC 20008

ATTICS AND HEIRLOOMS

Brackman, Barbara. *Clues in the Calico: Identifying and Dating Quilts*. McLean, VA: EPM Publications, 1989.

A quilt made by the hands of your ancestor can really bring history to life. Certain patterns, sewing styles, color choices, and material types act as identifying marks to the trained eye. Have a look at this book to understand more of what that quilt can tell you.

Earnest, Russell D. *Grandma's Attic: Making Heirlooms Part of Your Family History*. Albuquerque, NM: R. D. Earnest Assoc., 1991.

Letters and diaries aren't the only important things you'll find in a relative's storage area. This book helps you recognize the significance of other objects once owned by your ancestors, such as china, quilts, silver, and furniture.

Frost, Lenore, *Dating Family Photos, 1850–1920*. Essendon, Victoria: L. Frost, 1991.

Although the author is writing about Australia, her valuable tips on dating a photo by what the people in it are wearing is helpful as applied to the United States, too. The cut of waistlines and collars, the shape of bustles and hoop skirts, and the height of men's hats are the sort of clues given in this book.

Fry, Gladys-Marie. *Stitched from the Soul: Slave Quilts from the Antebellum South.* **New York: Dutton Studio Books, 1990.**

Humans' longing for freedom and their sorrow over life's suffering are expressed in every artform. Quilts made by African American slaves are especially beautiful and moving because—in a controlled, innocent-looking manner—they express some of the greatest sorrow known to humanity.

Leon, Eli. *Who'd a Thought It.* **San Francisco: San Francisco Craft and Folk Art Museum, 1987.**

This book gives the study of quilts a fascinating twist. It concerns itself not with the patterns and stitches learned from one generation to the next, but with the element of improvisation present in these works. Beautifully illustrated.

Simpson, Jeffrey. *The American Family: A History in Photographs.* **New York: Viking Press, 1976.**

Photography became popular in the United States after the Civil War. Looking through this moving volume will inspire you to hunt for photos of your family and to keep photos of yourself. They are an irreplaceable record of the past.

Wahlman, Maud. *Signs and Symbols: African Images in African American Quilts.* **New York: Studio Books, 1993.**

Slaves brought here directly from Africa in the seventeenth and eighteenth centuries carried with them memories of their peoples' traditional art forms. It is no surprise that those designs and aesthetics appear in their quilting patterns. Like other traditions in slave culture, quilt patterns and the devices used to make them were passed on from one generation to the next, so even those who had never seen Africa still used its images in their handiwork.

GRAVEYARDS

NOTE: Thousands of books describe or index specific graveyards or collection of cemeteries. Check for publications by the county where your ancestor is buried. If your library computer system allows it, search using the multiple key words "cemeteries" or "gravestones" plus the county name.

The African Burial Ground. New York: Municipal Archives of the City of New York, 1994.

This is a booklet that accompanied an exhibit. Featured are photographs of tombstones from the African American cemetery excavated near New York City. It has been a source of pride for New York blacks to organize to preserve this site and the heritage it represents.

The American Cemetery. Chicago: Prettyman Publishing.

This monthly periodical provides information on graveyards around the country, including historical landmarks and recent excavations.

**The Association for Gravestone Studies
46 Plymouth Road
Needham, MA 02192**

Write to this association for a free brochure describing their publications about gravestones and cemeteries.

Jacobs, Walker G. *Stranger Stop and Cast an Eye: A Guide to Gravestones and Gravestone Rubbing*. Brattleboro, VT: S. Greene Press, 1973.

Learn to recognize symbolism in a gravestone's decorations, as well as understanding the importance of dates and verses. Illustrated with photos of rubbings from New

England, this book also teaches practical techniques for making clear rubbings.

Nishiura, Elizabeth. *American Battle Monuments*. Detroit: Omnigraphics, 1989.

Many African Americans fought in the two World Wars. This is a guide to military cemeteries and monuments maintained by the American Battle Monuments Commission.

Rose, Jerome C., ed. *Gone to a Better Land: A Biohistory of a Rural Black Cemetery in the Post-Reconstruction South*. Fayetteville: Arkansas Archaeological Survey, 1985.

Focuses on the cemetery called Cedar Grove Site in Lafayette County, Arkansas. The excavators of this nineteenth-century graveyard have been able to gather together quite a tale by studying tombstone inscriptions, human remains, and other clues.

Sluby, Paul E., and Wormley, Stanton L. *Records of the Columbian Harmony Cemetery, Washington, DC*. Washington, DC: Columbian Harmony Society, 1993.

This seven-volume set includes all known burial records since 1831 for this major African American cemetery. Sluby and Wormley have published other such compilations about Washington, DC graveyards.

Taylor, Anne Hatcher. *Black Cemetery Records, Reunions, and Personality Sketches: Hertford and Gates Counties, North Carolina, 1850–1988*. Winton, NC: Hatcher-Taylor Press, 1988.

The Carolinas have had among the largest populations of African Americans since the nineteenth century. If your ancestors were among those residents, a register such as this one is very useful. You can even trace more recent relations in this book.

ORAL TRADITION

Barber, Karin, and de Moraes Farias, P. F., eds.
Discourse and Its Disguises: The Interpretation of African Oral Texts. **Birmingham, U.K.: Centre of West African Studies, Birmingham University, 1989.**

When animals appear in African traditional tales, often each creature stands for a certain human characteristic. This is one example of how things are not always what they seem in African oral texts. Sometimes picturesque images and funny stories can be metaphors for serious social commentary.

Feelings, Muriel. *Grio: The Praise Singer.* **Philadelphia: Enteracom, Inc., 1985.**

The African *grio* (or *griot*) is the traditional historian and archivist for his or her community. This book explores the functions of the *grio* as collective memory, collective voice, entertainer, and ego-stroker to the rich and powerful.

Glaser, Marlies, and Pausch, Marion, eds.
Caribbean Writers: Between Orality and Writing. **Atlanta: Editions Rodopi, 1994.**

The oral tradition traveled to the Caribbean with Africans brought there as slaves. In this new location it took on a character of its own, but never completely left behind its African roots. Articles include "Oral Tradition and Recent Caribbean Poetry" by E. Rodriguez and "The Black Writer in the Multicultural Caribbean" by C. Bodunde. Some articles are in French.

Laye, Camara. *The Guardian of the Word (Kouma Lafolo Kouma).* **Translated by James Kirkup. New York: Vintage Books, 1984.**

Translated from the French *Le Maître de la Parole*, this book discusses the past and present social role of the *griot*, or storyteller, among the Mandingo people of West Africa.

Miller, Joseph C., ed. *The African Past Speaks: Essays on Oral Tradition and History.* **Hamden, CT: Archon, 1980.**

How much history can you actually learn from oral historians? This book considers that topic, along with the oral culture's definition of the word "history," which is very different from its definition in a literate culture.

Mphahlele, Es'kia. *Poetry and Humanism: Oral Beginnings.* **Johannesburg: Witwatersrand University Press, 1986.**

The basic concept behind this paper is that Africa is not the only culture for which oral tradition has been a mainstay in education and the arts. Even western Europe, which has prided itself on its literary accomplishments since the Renaissance, was able to flower into its written glory only because of a strong tradition of oral literature dating from the early Middle Ages.

Nandwa, Jane, and Bukenya, Austin. *African Oral Literature for Schools.* **Nairobi: Longman Kenya, 1983.**

Oral history and other kinds of traditional verse are an integral part of every indigenous African culture. This book suggests that it makes sense to include oral literature as part of African children's education, now that the Western school system has taken over from traditional community teaching methods.

Noss, Phillip A., ed. *The Ancestors' Beads.* **Hamilton, New Zealand: Outrigger, 1989.**

This collection of six essays on African folk literature is a special publication of *Crosscurrents* magazine. It considers such issues as rhythm patterns, formulaic verses and motives, and the participation of the community in an oral performance.

Obiechina, Emmanuel N. *Language and Theme: Essays on African Literature.* **Washington, DC: Howard University Press, 1990.**

Although oral history always incorporates a large degree of improvisation, there are certain words, phrases, even entire verses that the *griot* or other oral performer has at his or her command to fill in or spice up a part of the story. These essays consider the use of words by oral historians.

Okpewho, Isidore. *African Oral Literature: Backgrounds, Character, and Continuity.* **Bloomington: Indiana University Press, 1992.**

An introduction to African oral history by a respected scholar on the subject. Included are the ancient history of the oral art forms, as well as their use in today's Africa and in the diaspora.

————. *Myth in Africa: A Study of Its Aesthetic and Cultural Relevance.* **New York: Cambridge University Press, 1983.**

Until the Muslims and Christians began to intermingle with traditional cultures in Africa, people in the community were taught history and survival skills by means of oral stories, proverbs, and verses. This book considers how oral history is partly art and entertainment and partly a people's archives.

Okpewho, Isidore, ed. *The Oral Performance in Africa.* **Ibadan: Spectrum Books, 1990.**

The performance of oral histories and tales is not a passive experience for the audience. The storyteller sings or chants the tale and is constantly interrupted, encouraged, bribed, reproached, and otherwise helped out by community members shouting out suggestions or throwing gifts and money.

Torrence, Jackie. *Traditions: A Potpourri of Tales.* **Rounder Records, 1994.**

Although this CD is intended for young children, Torrence's storytelling technique will charm listeners of all ages. This African American woman proves by her gifted and loving recordings that the art of spinning yarns to delight and teach is still alive and well.

Vansina, Jan. *Oral Tradition as History.* **Madison: University of Wisconsin Press, 1985.**

Knowing how to listen to oral history takes a lot of study. This is an introduction to study of oral literature, knowing how much to take literally, how to recognize patterns and motifs, and the importance of improvisation.

Warner, Keith Q. *Kaiso! The Trinidad Calypso.* **Washington, DC: Three Continents Press, 1982.**

Calypso is the folk music of Trinidad and Tobago. The author considers this exciting musical form to be a continuation of the ancient African tradition of oral literature.

Wright, Donald R. *Oral Traditions from the Gambia.* **Athens: Ohio University Center for International Studies, Africa Program, 1979–80.**

This two-volume set includes portraits and useful maps, as well as an extensive bibliography. The first volume discusses the Mandinka *griots*; the second discusses family elders.

Chapter 5
The Census, and What It Doesn't Tell

One of the most important sources that can be found at (or ordered through) a research library is the federal census. Once you have found some names of relatives from recent generations, it is time to verify where and when they lived, and to look for more. The census is the place to start.

In all stages of genealogy, the best way to proceed is backward in time. Document and confirm recent events and generations, then take one step back to what came just before. The same is true of the census: Start with the most recent, then go to the previous decades.

To protect the privacy of living citizens, the federal government maintains censuses as classified documents until they are at least seventy years old. The most recent publicized census is that from 1920.

To use the 1920 census, start with its index, not the original census itself. While the original is organized by county, the indexes are condensed by entire state. Get the index for the state in which you believe some of your relatives lived in that year. Under the surname you will find all the individuals with that name in that state. Each entry will tell which county's complete census you should check for more details, along with the page and line number where that individual appears.

The index is written in a space-saving code called Soundex. You look up the initial letter of the surname. Any consonant sounds after that are coded phonetically by number. Vowels and the letters H and Y are not represented. The code works as follows. The number 1 represents the letters B, P, F, V. The number 2 stands for the letters C, S, K, G, J, Q, X, Z. The number 3 stands for D and T.

The number 4 represents L; the number 5 equals M and N, the number 6 is R. In the Soundex, the name "Johnson" would appear as J525.

When you learn something in the census, be sure to check it against other documents and sources you have. The census is notorious for errors—partly because of clerical mistakes, but mostly because citizens tend not to answer the census accurately.

The great majority of blacks in America before the Civil War were slaves. Slaves were not considered citizens. They were denied the most basic legal rights, such as the right to marry. They were not even allowed the dignity of having a surname. In the censuses from 1860 back to the first one in 1790, slaves are listed under their masters, merely as "Negro" plus a first name. A person who had been a slave but who got his freedom was listed as an individual with a surname beginning in the first census following his release.

Even after the Civil War, it took the rest of the century for the censuses to begin offering reliable information about blacks. Part of the problem was the difficulty in documenting black households. Most slaves released after Abolition had no idea where to go to find work; they had no money, few friends, and very little confidence that they were actually safe from being recaptured. As a result, these people moved all over the country and changed households frequently. The 1870 census, the first one after the Civil War, does not list the relationships of people within households. It is therefore easy to assume mistakenly that a group of people made up a nuclear family, when in fact they may not have been related.

As slaves, black people were allowed only a first name, usually assigned to them from the Judeo-Christian tradition. When four million slaves were freed by the Thirteenth Amendment, all of those people had to choose surnames.

It is a common assumption that most slaves adopted their former master's surname when they were freed. On the contrary, it has been estimated that 95 percent of those four million slaves freed after the Civil War chose names other than their former owners'. There is a clear reason for this.

Many slave families chose their own surnames after emancipation.

Emancipation meant a slave's chance to make a new beginning as a free human being, without ties to his or her horrible past in servitude. To adopt a former master's surname meant to make that past a permanent, legal part of one's life. There was also a strong fear that this freedom would soon be taken away. Blacks wanted to obliterate ties with former owners so that they would not be sent back and receive brutal punishment if slavery became legal again.

Where, then, did African Americans find suitable surnames? The vast majority chose white, Christian names rather than African ones. This was not some sort of sell-out on their part. Having a "normal-sounding" name was a bare necessity for getting a toehold in American society. Suddenly a group of people who had been regarded as little more than animals were sent forth as citizens. Former slave owners looked at an African American and thought, "slave." Taking a "white" name helped stave off a little of this blatant prejudice.

Fortunately for genealogists, former slaves did tend to choose surnames related in some way to their past. They might pick the surname of a grandparent's master, the maiden name of their own master's wife, or the name of someone who had done them a good turn. Mulattoes often took the surname of a white relative. Some people chose to name themselves after heroes like George Washington and Thomas Jefferson.

As you work backward through the decades in the census, you may come to a point when your ancestors seem to disappear. Tracking your kin in the decades after the Civil War is a tricky business for many reasons. During that period things can get confusing. For one thing, some people moved around a lot and changed their surname at each place of residence. There are cases of people changing their names periodically over a stretch of twenty years. Another factor is that most freed slaves were illiterate and often did not know basic vital statistics about themselves.

Slave owners kept their slaves in ignorance in an attempt to solidify their power as masters. They feared that allowing slaves to learn reading and writing would help them to articulate their outrage against the inhumane system of slavery.

Most newly freed slaves, therefore, could not write the surname they chose. Many could not even spell their first name. This has a strange effect on the census. In two consecutive decades you may find an ancestor's name so changed that it is unrecognizable. Census takers would mishear names, be told wrong names, or record nicknames instead of proper names. Isaac may become Isaiah from one census to the next, and Nancy may suddenly be listed by her nickname, Mimi. You will have to rely on outside sources— letters, legal documents, and newspaper clippings—to help straighten out these issues.

There were other impediments to an accurate census of blacks. For example, when members of a biological family had been split up as slaves or went their separate ways in freedom, not all the family members necessarily took the same surname. It was also common for slaves not to know their actual age and birthday, nor did they have documentation of their parentage. Children born to slave mothers became the legal property of the mother's owner. The actual father was not officially recognized, even if he took an active, loving role in the rearing of his child.

This should not be taken to mean that all blacks were illiterate. In the nineteenth century, before Emancipation, free blacks were known for a very high level of literacy. Many made it a point to help educate newly freed slaves. A few slaves were actually taught by their owners, who had at least that much compassion for their humanity. Others took the great risk of teaching themselves or finding missionaries or fellow slaves to teach them. If their owners found out they would be severely punished. Some slaves went for years pretending to be illiterate and uneducated, but in every furtive spare moment they studied the Bible, history books, and newspapers. It is also untrue that, because many blacks could not read white people's words, they were any less intelligent than other races. African Americans denied a Western education exercised their minds using the African oral traditions. Their developments in storytelling, humor, dance, and music—all now central to American pop culture—attest to their creative genius.

The kind of education and opportunity a slave had depended largely on his relationship with the owner. On plantations the situation was usually the worst. There were many more blacks than whites on a plantation, and owners' terror of rebellion convinced them of the need to keep their slaves "ignorant." On the other hand, many slaves worked on small farms or as household servants. In these cases blacks and whites tended to work side by side, sharing the load and getting to know one another. Slaves in this situation were more likely to be taught to read and sometimes formed positive relationships with members of the owner's family.

There were also slaves in the cities, especially in the

Southern states. Many of these people worked as skilled laborers and artisans, learning trades like silver- and blacksmithing, carpentry, painting, and shipbuilding. These talented workmen usually continued to practice their trade after Emancipation; often their children and grandchildren worked in the same profession.

A family trade can be a great hint for a genealogist. If you can figure out from censuses or other documents that more than one generation of a family worked in the same trade, that may be a clue to the skills and workplace of the most recent slave in your family tree.

If you are descended from blacks who were free during the nineteenth century, your search back to that era may be somewhat easier. As you look through the census, take note of every person with the same surname living in the same neighborhood. You can find out each household's street address in the census. It is a good idea, and also fun, to try to track down a historical map of that neighborhood and place those same-surname households on it. Maps and gazeteers of this sort can sometimes be obtained at local history libraries or county archives serving the area that you are studying. Don't assume that everyone with the same surname is related. Just keep the option open as you go.

Local directories, stored in state or local archives, are similar to the census. However, they list only the residents of the particular town, give more information about each individual, and are updated annually. If you can find a directory for the area you're looking into, it can help pinpoint certain events. For example, if a family appears in the 1872 directory, but not in the one from 1871, you can assume that the family moved to the area during that twelve-month period, or that the head of the household changed his or her surname during that time. Be forewarned that many of these directories, especially from before the Civil War, list free blacks separately from whites (slaves are not entered as individuals at all). In Northern directories, blacks tend to be listed along with whites, but are marked with asterisks—a more subtle form of prejudice.

A freedman's document of release is a good piece of evidence to have. These papers, called deeds of manumission, or manumission records, state that a certain person has been set free, or else promise that he or she will be released at a certain time or under certain circumstances. Look for them in special collections and archives in the state where the ancestor was a slave. The deed of manumission may be filed under the ex-slave's new surname or under the owner's name.

The luckiest genealogists are those who can get their hands on the most legal documents. This is no easy task for someone searching for African American roots. Sit down at your typewriter or computer and get ready to write some letters. Following clues you've garnered from talking to relatives and using the census, you want to request documents that verify information that you think is true.

From the courthouse for the county in which an ancestor lived, you can request birth, marriage, and death certificates. You will be sent an official form to fill out and will be required to provide as much information as possible about the ancestor and the event in question. The further back into the nineteenth century you go, the more likely that any vital records on your ancestor will be kept at the state, rather than county, archive—if any such records exist at all. Governmental records on slaves were scanty at best. Remember that slaves were not citizens and could not even legally marry. Even after the Civil War, the maintenance of records on blacks was not taken very seriously, and they were almost always separate from whites' records. When you write to the county for records, you might also ask about local history books on that area. Sometimes such publications can lead to valuable information on the residents and their activities.

Interracial Unions

Some people find that a few of their ancestors are not nearly so difficult to trace—because they were white. This is one of the most shocking things that black people sometimes discover as they trace their roots. A person who thinks of himself as a pure African American may find that his great-grandmother was the daughter of a black woman and her white owner, or that his grandfather's great uncle married a white woman when he came North. Literally millions of blacks in America today have at least one non-African ancestral line.

Frederick Douglass, the great abolitionist, was himself a first-generation mulatto, born of a black mother and a white father, and his second wife was a white woman. Many people, both white and black, were scandalized, but Douglass could not understand what the fuss was about. After all, the concept behind his struggle toward Emancipation was that blacks and whites were equal and should be able to interact as fellow citizens.

By far the most common parentage of early mulatto babies was a male slave owner and a female slave. That woman rarely had any choice in the matter. The fact that her owner forced her to sleep with him constitutes rape, whether or not the encounter was violent.

Not all interracial relationships were forced. It was not uncommon for freed blacks, especially men, to join up with a white partner in the more tolerant North. In certain geographical areas interracial marriages were common. For example, in the eighteenth century Jamaican blacks and Irish immigrants to Jamaica often intermarried. Many of those couples or their offspring subsequently moved to America. Another common interracial union was between blacks and Native Americans. This was so widespread, in fact, that by the 1800s very few of the Eastern American indigenous groups had any "pure-bloods" left. The Creek and Seminole peoples mixed frequently with African Americans.

Thousands of babies were born to interracial unions. The children ranged in color from the deepest brown to ivory. A social scale developed among mulattoes in which those with the fairest complexion became the elite. There were even exclusive clubs for light mulattoes. One, the Blue Vein Society, accepted only members pale enough that their veins showed blue through their skin.

Frederick Douglass, a former slave who became a leading abolitionist, was the product of an interracial union.

Mulattoes, no matter how fair and no matter how full of white blood, were still considered "Negro" by law and public opinion. Blacks born with fair skin often tried to "pass" as white. Under the pretense of having no black blood, they would travel, get jobs, marry whites, and use public facilities and services unavailable to people darker than themselves. Skin bleaching and hair straightening were attempted to "whiten" people to the point of passing. Blacks were often jealous of relatives and friends who could pass. Nevertheless, they rarely gave those lucky ones away. The punishments for getting caught as a "fake" white included marriage annulment, loss of employment, heavy fines, and jail.

Interracial unions and the presence of another race in one's family tree are troubling for some people. However, the practical genealogist has to take every piece of information she finds and turn it to her advantage. Have you found traces of white blood from the early nineteenth century or even earlier? This may mean that you have at least one family line for which there are good records. And you never know what information about one branch of your family tree will yield clues about other branches.

Resources

Bureau of the Census
Pittsburg, KS 66762

This is where to write for information on censuses not yet released to the public (since 1920). They'll send you a form and a list of fees.

Dollarhide, William, and Thorndale, William.
Map Guide to the U.S. Federal Censuses, 1790–1920.
Baltimore: Genealogical Publishing, 1987.

This guide shows what areas are covered in surviving censuses. Very useful if you know the general area but not the exact town where an ancestor lived.

Eichholz, Alice, and Rose, James M. *Free Black Heads of Households in the New York State Federal Census, 1790–1830.* **Detroit: Gale Research Co., 1981.**

If your African American ancestors settled in New York State, this is a really helpful resource. The editors have gone through the census for all of the counties in New York and compiled all of the information on blacks listed as heads of household. It can save you a lot of searching through the Soundex, and it includes censuses for which some records are now destroyed.

Health Resources Administration
National Center for Health Statistics
Rockville, MD 20852

Write for a form to order certificates or records of ancestors who were U.S. citizens but who died or were born in a foreign country.

Kemp, Thomas Jay. *International Vital Records Handbook.* **Baltimore: Genealogical Publishing, 1990.**

Was your great-great-grandfather a manager for the British East India company so that your great-grandmother was born in Bangladesh? Don't worry; check this source for how to find unusual records relating to Great Britain, Canada, and the United States.

Kirkham, E. Kay. *How to Read the Handwriting and Records of Early America.* **Salt Lake City: Deseret Book, 1965.**

Before the advent of typewriters, legal documents were written by hand. Even when they were prepared by someone with really good handwriting (which was often *not* the case), there were many differences in penmanship practices between the eighteenth century and now, making key words difficult to decipher.

Lawson, Sandra M. *Generations Past: A Selected List of Sources for Afro-American Genealogical Research.* **Washington, DC: Library of Congress, 1988.**

The Library of Congress has a strong collection on genealogy for all ethnicities. This is a publication by one of their staff members, describing how to use the LC archives to trace freedmen and slave roots.

Matthews, Harry Bradshaw. *African American Genealogical Research: How to Trace Your Family History.* **Baldwin, NY: Matthews Heritage Services, 1992.**

A good introduction to black genealogy by someone who has spent decades practicing the skill and teaching it to others. This manual is interesting because it traces a slave ancestor's chosen surname to Europe and finally to Egypt.

National Archives
General Reference Branch
Washington, DC 20408

Write for forms needed to order photocopies of specific pages of a census.

National Archives Trust Fund
P.O. Box 100793
Atlanta, GA 30384

Write to inquire about purchasing particularly useful censuses on microform and CD-ROM.

National Archives and Records Administration
Washington, DC 20408

Write for free catalogs of their publications and microfilms. This is the storehouse for censuses, vital records, and many other documents essential to genealogists.

National Archives Regional Archives
Central Plains
2312 East Bannister Road
Kansas City, MO 64131
816-926-6272

Information on Iowa, Kansas, Missouri, Nebraska.

Great Lakes
7358 South Pulaski Road
Chicago, IL 60629
312-581-7816

Information on Illinois, Indiana, Michigan, Minnesota, Ohio, Wisconsin.

Mid-Atlantic
Ninth and Market Streets, Room 1350
Philadelphia, PA 19107
215-597-3000

Information on Delaware, Maryland, Pennsylvania, Virginia, West Virginia.

New England
380 Trapelo Road

Waltham, MA 02154
617-647-8100

Information on Connecticut, Maine, Massachusetts, New Hampshire, Rhode Island, Vermont.

Northeast
Building 22-MOT Bayonne
Bayonne, NJ 07002-5388
210-823-7252

Information on New Jersey, New York, Puerto Rico, Virgin Islands.

Pacific Northwest
6125 Sand Point Way NE
Seattle, WA 98115
206-526-6507

Information on Alaska, Idaho, Oregon, Washington state.

Pacific Sierra
1000 Commodore Drive
San Bruno, CA 94066
415-876-9009

Information on Hawaii, Nevada, northern California.

Pacific Southwest
24000 Avila Road
P.O. Box 6719
Laguna Niguel, CA 92677-6719
714-643-4241

Information on Arizona, southern California, Nevada's Clark County.

Rocky Mountain
Building 48, Denver Federal Center
Denver, CO 80225
303-236-0818

Information on Colorado, Montana, North Dakota, South Dakota, Utah, Wyoming.

Southwest
501 West Felix Street
P.O. Box 6216
Fort Worth, TX 76115
817-334-5525

Information on Arkansas, Louisiana, New Mexico, Oklahoma, Texas.

Streets, David H. *Slave Genealogy: A Research Guide with Case Studies.* **Bowie, MD: Heritage Books, 1986.**

The introductory chapters in this book are a good overview of slavery and its effect on black genealogy. Most of the book is given over to case studies, actual genealogical searches described step by step.

Twenty Censuses: Population and Housing Questions, 1790–1980. **Orting, WA: Heritage Quest.**

The manner of listing blacks in the federal census altered as national laws and opinions changed. This distillation and description of certain kinds of information available from the United States censuses also explains how the gathering of information has changed over the centuries.

Where to Write for Vital Records: Births, Deaths, Marriages and Divorces.

Order this booklet from the U.S. Government Printing Office, Superintendent of Documents, Washington, DC 20402. It costs $3.25. Write for a brochure of publications relating to family research.

Chapter 6
Searching for Slaves

One of the most frustrating ironies of slavery's legacy is one that haunts genealogists in particular. Because slaves were not allowed literacy and kept their own histories by oral methods, there are almost no letters or diaries in their own hands. Because they were not citizens and were not even allowed to marry, there are practically no legal or official records on them as individuals. Hard as it is to accept, the best place to turn for information on slaves is to do research on their owners.

To begin this process, it is necessary to know the name of at least one slaveholder involved with your ancestors. You can try to get this name from oral histories passed on by your relatives, from letters and diaries (usually written after Emancipation), or from deeds of manumission filed under the freed slave's name.

The necessary documents are usually found at the county courthouse serving the area where the owner lived. A good place to start is with his or her will. As part of the owner's property, slaves were willed to relatives or friends—or granted their freedom—as a condition of the owner's final testament. Keep in mind that in all of these documents the slaves will be referred to only by their first names (Negro John, for example). Write down every slave mentioned, since you never know who may turn out to be a relative of yours. Also note the owner's relatives mentioned in the will and look at documents for some of these people. Often various members of an extended white family would own members of an extended black family.

Besides visiting county courthouses or writing to them with your requests, there is another way to access slave owners' records. The Family History Library in Salt Lake City, Utah, operated by The Church of Jesus Christ of Latter-day Saints (the Mormons), is the largest genealogical library in the world. They have published a microfiche collection of vital and legal documents. This International Genealogy Index (IGI) includes 150 million persons who died between 1500 and 1875. The collection is especially strong in the histories of people of British heritage, which describes a majority of American slaveholders. Family History Library has branches all over the United States (write for a list). From these branches you can order the microfiche you need.

The American Genealogical Lending Library is another potential source, particularly for wills. They can provide to their members transcripts of wills and some estate records. By writing to the AGLL, 593 West North Street, Bountiful, UT 84011, or by contacting the librarian at a local research library, you can request such transcripts.

County Deed Books

Each county keeps a record of legal deeds transacted at the county level. To use a deed book properly, it is necessary to visit the county courthouse or the state archive where the deed records are kept.

Records kept as county deeds include the following:

- Estate records. These list all of a landowner's property, including slaves.
- Prenuptial agreements. When two families who owned land became connected by marriage, they often wrote out a contract stating how property would be divided during the marriage and in the event that it should end. Slaves are sometimes listed in these agreements.
- Deeds of gifts. These are legal documentation of the change of ownership.
- Deeds of hire. Deeds of hire record what the job was, who owned the slave, who was renting him, and for how long. The slave's name, sex, and age might be given.
- Mortgage deeds. Mortgage deeds record circum-

stances where slaves were used as security for loans.

- Bills of sale. A slave might be sold off an estate for a variety of reasons. Bills of sale included where and when the sale took place, the names of the seller and buyer and their counties of residence, the market value of the slave, and perhaps the slave's name, age, and sex.

Colored Troops

African American soldiers have served in the military in every war since the American Revolution. Some were freed-men who volunteered to help a country they hoped to improve. Some were slaves who volunteered because they thought that doing so would buy their freedom; usually they were disappointed. As the Civil War began, the Yankees' ranks were full of blacks, both free and fugitive. Slaves would escape just to join the fight, in hope that soon they would all be free.

Any federal or state-supported military troop had records, although not all survived. Sometimes a person who served in the army while still a slave appears in no records other than his military registration and his pension record. Those are enough, though, to help a genealogist.

From the Civil War, records exist for 180,000 "colored troops" (soldiers' regiments were segregated by race) and 29,000 black sailors. It is estimated that 80 percent of those people had escaped from slavery to join the Northern forces. Most of the records on blacks serving in the Revolutionary War have been destroyed. There were 5,000 of these black patriots, almost all of them foot soldiers. They were registered by their first name, plus "Negro," an ironic insult to people offering to defend their new country with their lives. There were a few exceptions, such as Samuel Waldon, a black man who gained the Army's respect as a ship's pilot.

The National Archives in Washington, DC is the place to turn for military records. A regional National Archives branch or a nearby research library will be able to order microfilm of the documents you need. Start with the General Index of U.S. Colored Troops. These list the name of the soldier, county of residence, rank, and any special notation. Pension records are included in this index. A military pension is paid to a soldier after duty, or to his widow after his death. Pension records can be a great way to learn the name and age of an ancestor's wife and children.

There are two useful lists from the late nineteenth century: from 1883, a list of U.S. veterans, and from 1890, a census of veterans and their widows. These can yield valuable information, but they are useful only if you know the county in which the veteran or his family lived at the time the census was compiled.

Early Black Organizations

Slaves were able to find friends and advocates in some denominations of the Christian church that did missionary work in the South. Before states began passing laws against it, missionaries taught blacks to read and write. This sometimes continued quietly even after such laws were passed. Also against the law in some states were integrated congregations, yet in 1782 there are records of Baptist and Lutheran churches holding illegal interracial services.

The Baptists and Catholics had much contact with blacks in slavery and are good sources of baptismal, marriage, and burial records. The Quakers were not only at the forefront of the Abolition movement, but also are famous for their excellent recordkeeping and archiving. Many other church records from before the Civil War are lost, but Quaker records are remarkably intact from that period.

A German sect called the Moravians did a great deal of practical work to help slaves out of their situation. Moravian activists purchased slaves themselves with the express purpose of releasing them. They would then give these former slaves basic education and jobs.

All of the Christian denominations to which blacks responded favorably eventually formed all-black congregations, led by black ministers. These provided not only a secure house of worship for African Americans, but also a focal

African American churches are often a major force in a community and may hold valuable records. Here the Metropolitan Community Church Choir in Chicago practices in 1948.

point around which a strong black community could evolve.

The first black-founded church was started by free blacks in Philadelphia in 1787. Called the Mother Bethel African Methodist Episcopal Church, it existed to aid, guide, and comfort the African American community. It published a newspaper called the *Christian Recorder*. Many editions of this publication have been preserved on microfilm.

During the late eighteenth and nineteenth centuries free blacks established small towns, mostly in the Northeast. The communities were known as "Guinea Towns" (the word *guinea* was often used in the North to refer to blacks). They became sanctuaries for newly released African Americans after the Civil War.

The most famous and moving example of free blacks aiding their brethren is the Underground Railroad, which helped 100,000 slaves escape before the Civil War. You may well have an ancestor who was saved on the Railroad. Unfortunately for genealogists and historians, the very nature of the Railroad made it essential that there be no written records of its activities. There is one fascinating book, from 1872, of Railroad records. It was compiled by Railroad worker William Still, who apparently wanted his organization's work preserved to inspire future generations. His *Underground Railroad* includes the names of those fugitives he helped, a physical description of each one, and even transcriptions of some conversations between Still and the fugitives.

Another kind of railroad is important to black genealogists. Fortunately, this one kept good records. This was the U.S. railway system, which employed thousands of African Americans after Reconstruction. By 1917 there were 150,000 blacks working in some aspect of railway service. Records from the U.S. Railroad Retirement Board are a treasure chest for family historians. Files on employees include not only information about the worker himself, but also his family: both the wife or children who claimed his pension and the worker's parents. You can write for information on a specific relative to:

U.S. Railroad Retirement Board
Bureau of Research
844 Rush Street
Chicago, IL 60611

The Free African Society was established in 1787. It existed to offer material assistance to freed blacks, including health care and burial insurance. Although many of these records have been destroyed, some still exist in state historical archives.

The Western Sanitary Commission was set up by the federal government at the close of the Civil War. It focused on North and South Carolina, helping blacks find jobs and places to live. Records on this organization can be found in the National Archives.

There were great hopes for a commission called the Freedman's Bureau, short for Bureau of Refugees, Freedmen, and Abandoned Land. Established in 1865, the Freedman's Bureau got off to a good start. It provided many useful services to ex-slaves. One of these was the Cohabitation Certificate, which legalized marriages that had occurred during slavery. The adjustment to freedom was not easy for some. Many male slaves, like their forebears in Africa since ancient times, had taken two or three wives at once. The federal government imposed Western Christian morals on those men, and made them choose only one of their wives as their legal partner.

The Freedman's Bureau never lived up to its potential. It failed to appropriate land to ex-slaves in the South, as it had intended. By 1869 it had practically stopped functioning, and three years later it officially shut down. Records from the Freedman's Bureau are available from the National Archives on microfilm.

Here are a few more organizations that served African Americans after the Civil War:

> New England Freedman's Aid Society
> National Freedman's Relief Association (New York and Washington, DC)
> Contraband Relief Association of Cincinnati (also called Western Freedman's Commission)
> Women's Aid Association (Philadelphia)
> American Freedmen's Union Commission
> American Missionary Association (Atlantic Coast, and along the Mississippi River)
> Freedman's Land and Home Society (Charleston, SC)
> Freedmen's Saving Bank (Augusta, GA)

Working Back Toward the Middle Passage

If you've made it back to the era when your ancestors were slaves, you deserve a big "Congratulations!" It takes hard work, creativity, and patience to trace an African American family line back that far. It also takes luck.

This does not compare with the amount of luck it will take to go further back in time from there. The next step is to find out when your "original immigrant ancestor" was brought to America, where he or she landed, and whether he or she was brought from Africa, South America, or the West Indies. Bear in mind that trying to get these answers is a wild game of chance. It also requires a lot of time and funds for travel.

But it's worth a try if you have the resources, so here's how to proceed. First you need to find your earliest ancestor for whom there are any records. You then need the earliest possible bill of sale for this person. Look for the document that tells when your ancestor was sold to that owner. Was that his first owner? The only way to find out is to investigate the seller listed on the receipt.

You will recall that a bill of sale usually gives the county of residence of both the buyer and seller. Go to the county deed books that contain documents on the seller's estate. (This will probably require travel to another county courthouse, possibly in another state.) Who was this person? A former owner of your ancestor? Or a trader or middleman? If the person was a former owner, repeat the process: Find the bill of sale documenting when your ancestor was sold to that person, and investigate the new seller.

Eventually, if all the records are preserved, you will come upon a merchant who bought your ancestor at a port or via interstate trade. Once you find a trader, it is likely to get very tricky. Unlike an owner, who would buy only a few slaves at once, a trader may have papers on hundreds in any given year.

You want to find out at which slave port your ancestor disembarked. The main American ports for slave ships were Newport, Rhode Island; New York City; Boston, Massachusetts; Baltimore, Maryland; Roanoke, Virginia; Philadelphia, Pennsylvania; and Savannah, Georgia.

Once you have a pretty good idea of where the ship docked, you'll want to figure out what company ran the ship, who was on it, where it came from, and where it stopped along the way. The only hope is that maritime logs still exist for that ship, and some description of the "cargo" (that is, the slaves) showing that your ancestor was aboard.

Those ship records that still exist can be found in state

and local historical societies, maritime archives near the port, or at the National Archives and Library of Congress. It may take a lot of letter writing to find the ones you need. The National Archives stores the logs of ships caught in illegal slave traffic. This can be a great resource. Unfortunately, only a tiny percentage of pirate slaving ships were ever caught. Lloyd's of London, the venerable insurance company, was the main insurer of slave ships that went to the British colonies. They published a newsletter, called *Lloyd's Register*, about the ships they insured and where they sailed. These include only some late-seventeenth- and eighteenth-century British ships, however.

It can help tremendously if you know some of your ancestor's physical characteristics. A ship's log or slave trader's record might remark on unusual traits such as missing or disfigured limbs, unusual (uneven) skin coloring, scars, tattoos, ritual scarification, traditional hairstyles, and missing or sharpened teeth. If you do take the plunge and try to find your ancestor's African home, such attributes can be valuable hints about which region or peoples to consider first.

Resources

GENERAL REFERENCES AND INDEXES

Beers, Henry Putney. *The Confederacy: A Guide to the Archives of the Confederate States of America.* **Washington, DC: National Archives and Records Administration, 1986.**

> The National Archives is one of the best sources for both historical and genealogical information concerning the South during the Civil War.

***Genealogical Periodical Annual Index.* Bowie, MD: Heritage Books.**

> The periodicals indexed here offer articles on every aspect of genealogy. A large research library may have this extensive index on CD-ROM.

Immigration and Naturalization Service Washington, DC 20536

> Naturalization records after 1906 are available here. Write for an order form.

Kaminkow, Marion J. *Genealogies in the Library of Congress: A Bibliography.* **Baltimore: Magna Carta, 1972.**

> There is no better introduction to the family histories available in the Library of Congress than this two-volume work. It lists books about research, family histories (by surname), army, pension, and other federal records.

———. *A Complement to Genealogies in the Library of Congress.* **Baltimore: Magna Carta, 1981.**

An update to the Library of Congress collection.

**Military Personnel Records
9700 Page Boulevard
St. Louis, MO 63132**

Ask for Standard Form 180, "Request Pertaining to Military Records," for information on the Army (after 1912), Navy (after 1885), or Marines (after 1895).

National Union Catalog of Manuscript Collections.
Washington, DC: Library of Congress, 1962.

Known as NUCMUC, this catalog will guide you to family histories, memoirs, and diaries that never reached publication. It represents only a tiny percentage of such manuscripts, but at least it's a start.

**Neagles, James C. *Confederate Research Sources:
A Guide to Archive Collections.* Salt Lake City, UT:
Ancestry Publishing, 1986.**

This guide covers all the confederate states and some border states. The vast majority of blacks who were brought to this country during the slaving years have some tie with the South.

**Parker, J. Carlyle. *Going to Salt Lake City to Do
Family History Research.* Turlock, CA: Marietta
Publishing, 1989.**

The central Family History Library has one of the best collections of records on African Americans from, during, and after the era of slavery. However, it can be an overwhelming place if you're not prepared. This guide offers advice on organizing and focusing your search before you go.

Periodical Source Index. **Fort Wayne, IN:
Allen County Public Library, Historical Genealogy
Department.**

Librarians call this index PERSI. It is updated annually. Entries are indexed by American place-name, Canadian place-name, family name, and document type.

LIBRARIES

Family History Library (FHL)
35 North West Temple Street
Salt Lake City, UT 84150

Affiliated with The Church of Jesus Christ of Latter-day Saints, this is the largest genealogical library in the world.

Fort Wayne Public Library
Historical Genealogy Collection
900 Webster Street
Fort Wayne, IN 46802

Because of its strength in Canadian family history, this library can be useful to those whose ancestors moved to the far north before the Civil War. That was a common destination for African Americans assisted by the Underground Railroad.

Free Library of Philadelphia
Logan Square
Philadelphia, PA 19141

Philadelphia was early a safe haven for fugitive slaves, and in the late eighteenth century it became a center for black beneficial organizations and churches.

Friends Historical Library
Swarthmore College
Swarthmore, PA 19081

Quakers were at the forefront of the Abolitionist movement. This Quaker-founded college holds a collection of information about the earliest Quakers in America.

New York Public Library
Local History and Genealogy Division
Fifth Avenue and 42nd Street
New York, NY 10018

This collection has good general information but is strongest in local history. Holds clipping files of towns, including photos. Good indexes to death notices.

Schomburg Center for Research in Black Culture
The New York Public Library
515 Malcolm X Boulevard
New York, NY 10037-1801

This is one of the best resources in the United States for African American studies of any kind. They encourage genealogical work and are equipped to help with the use of censuses and indexes.

Chapter 7
High-Tech Genealogy

In the past few decades it seems as though computers have gradually been taking over our world. Genealogy too is being caught up in the digital revolution. Some people began using computers to assist in genealogical research in the 1960s, but it is only recently that genealogists who are not technology experts have had the resources to benefit from the power of computers.

Computers offer a number of advantages to the genealogist. For starters, they really speed up tasks that need to be done over and over again.

Another computer benefit involves note-taking. If you can get your hands on a computer while the research is fresh in your mind, you can type your notes, print them out, save them on a disk, and throw away the notes.

Need to sort all your relatives by date or place of birth? A computer can do that in seconds. Are you writing a family history? A word processing program lets you correct your mistakes painlessly. Absolutely stuck tracing a family line? Hop onto the Internet, and get in touch with other genealogists who may be able to help you out, and whom you may be able to help in turn.

There are three basic types of software that are useful to the genealogist. *Database management* programs are the real workhorses. They allow you to input and store the information you gather, and also to organize, sort, and print out that information in various ways. *Word processing* programs allow you to store documents of any size. They are the most efficient way to write a story, biography, or family history. *Graphics* and *desktop publishing* software let you present your findings attractively.

Genealogical software packages take the functions they need from all three types of software. Descriptions of some of the better-known packages are given below. Be warned that many of them are rather expensive.

The Church of Jesus Christ of Latter-day Saints deals with more genealogical information than any other institution in the world. It's no surprise, then, to learn that they devised the first all-purpose genealogy software package, Personal Ancestral File (PAF). They also invented a file-format, Genealogical Data Communications (GEDCOM), that still reigns as the standard way of representing genealogical information in a computer. If you buy software, it's good idea to get a package that works in GEDCOM; there's a better chance that you'll be able to trade information with other computer genealogists. PAF has inspired several companies to market software of their own, but it's still a leader in the field and is continuously being updated. It consists of three parts. Family Records, the central piece, stores and organizes your information and prints out charts. The second piece, Research Data Files, lets you type in your research notes and keeps them organized. Finally, Genealogic Info Exchange translates files from other programs into GEDCOM so that PAF can use them. It also includes a computerized "manual" that guides you through the whole PAF package.

The Roots software package is a useful system with a couple of features that set it apart. The user can customize the data for each individual, including information not specifically covered in most packages. Roots has a quick way of copying information (say, a birthplace) from one ancestor's entry to anothers. And it surpasses all other packages in what you can print from it.

There are smaller, less expensive programs that can take some of the hassle out of the root-searching process. Generations Library is a database management system created especially for genealogical information. And if you're launching into writing a family history, or even just a biography of your most colorful ancestor, Biography Maker may be for you. It helps you think small as you tackle such a large project. Biography Maker also includes writing tips and hints on how to weave historical background into your story.

Programs like these are not the only way computers make life easier for the genealogist. New technology has also made vital records available on floppy disks, on CD-ROM, and over telephone lines. The American Genealogical Lending Library (AGLL) has electronic databases that you can search over the phone. The number is listed in **Resources** at the end of this chapter. Their databases include census, social security, and death records. AGLL is also in the process of compiling marriage records on floppy disk and census records on CD-ROM.

The growing popularity of the Internet and on-line services offers even more opportunities for genealogists. Several on-line services, including CompuServe and GEnie, have forums for genealogists. And all you need is a modem to access any of the many bulletin board services. There are general-purpose genealogy bulletin boards such as the National Genealogy Conference. The CENSOFT board keeps you up-to-date on the latest genealogical software. Other bulletin boards, called Genealogy Echoes, act as forums for specific genealogical topics. They often have worldwide access and have come up with a system, called the Tafel Matching System, that encodes surnames. People in search of information on a particular family can use the surname code to go straight to the part of the bulletin board where that surname can be found.

Computers' ability to store and manipulate vast amounts of information make them a perfect fit for genealogical research. And genealogists' love for sharing information will turn surfing the Internet into their favorite pastime.

Resources

FAMILY HISTORY ON COMPUTER

American Genealogical Lending Library (AGLL)
801-298-5446

> This organization offers excellent services to its members, including a search service. They are also up-to-date on technological innovations.

Ancestral File Operations Unit
50 East North Temple Street
Salt Lake City, UT 84150
801-240-2584

> Write for information on the Personal Ancestral File software and the GEDCOM compatibility system.

Banner Blue Software
P.O. Box 7865
Fremont, CA 94537
510-795-4490

> Write for information on their Biography Maker software.

Commsoft, Inc.
7795 Bell Road
Windsor, CA 95495-0130
800-327-6687

> Write for information on their Roots IV software.

Dollarhide Systems
203 Holly Street

Bellingham, WA 28225
206-671-3808

Write for information on their Everyone's Family Tree software for beginners.

LDB Association Inc.
Dept. Q, Box 20837
Wichita, KS 67208-6837
316-683-6200

Write for information on their Kin Write and KinPublish software.

Quinsept, Inc.
P.O. Box 216
Lexington, MA 02173
800-637-ROOT

Call (toll-free) or write for information on their Family Roots and Lineage software. Lineage is a lower-priced version of Family Roots. Separate GEDCOM software is necessary.

THE INTERNET

The following are the major commercial Internet access providers.

America Online
800-827-6364

CompuServe
800-848-8990

GEnie
800-638-9636

Prodigy Services Co.
800-PRODIGY

Chapter 8
Nontraditional Families and Family Issues

Researching your family history can make you feel part of a larger community, a family community as well as a cultural community. But it's very difficult for a researcher to start without the names of his most immediate ancestors: his biological parents and grandparents. If you are being raised by adoptive parents or by a single parent, you may well find yourself faced with this roadblock, but it needn't prevent you from proceeding.

When a young person wants to know about an absent parent in order to research family history, he or she should talk to the single parent. Discussing the absent parent can bring up painful feelings for the single parent, who may be interested in leaving the past behind. A good approach can be to start out slowly, with brief conversations about the "other" parent every so often. This gives the single parent the chance to get used to the son's or daughter's curiosity about the absent parent. The young person can also make it clear that he or she is interested in making a family tree, and not in abandoning one parent for the other.

What can an adopted person do? The records concerning the biological parents of an adopted child are "sealed" by law until the child turns eighteen years of age. This law was passed to protect those parents who don't want to be found by the child they gave up, as well as adoptive parents who don't want their adopted child to locate her original parents. If the adoptee is thought to be at risk for a serious genetic illness, the records can be legally unsealed. The doctor and adoptive parents must get a court order to access the biological parents' medical history.

Often adoptees are merely curious about their biological parents and family origins. It's a perfectly normal and reasonable curiosity, but usually difficult to satisfy. Until she is eighteen, an adoptee can't look at her parents' sealed records. A good first step for someone in this situation is to talk to the adoptive parents. Adoptive parents often become anxious when their child expresses curiosity about her first parents. You may not have an interest in researching your birth family. Perhaps you feel that your adoptive family is the only family you want to know anything about. If this is the case, you may want to research the family history of your adoptive family. After all, you're a part of the same family now, too. A child and her adoptive parents should talk about feelings and potential outcomes before the child tries to find her original parents.

An adopted child may be able to get a start on genealogical research without ever meeting her birth mother. By telling her parents she is interested in putting together a family tree, she can set them at ease so they'll be comfortable lending a hand. Moreover, public records such as the census cannot be withheld from minors. When the adopted child turns eighteen, it will be easier for her to do genealogical research because of her experience.

Besides access to these records, the magical age of eighteen also allows people to sign up on adoption registers. If the biological parents have also signed up, they'll be matched up with their child. In addition, all over the world, groups are working on behalf of adoptees, trying to make the search for original parents a little easier.

Adoptees who have succeeded in tracing their roots have the following advice for those in a similar situation:

- Be patient. Legally, you can't unseal the records of your biological family until you've turned eighteen. (The only exception is by a court order issued on medical grounds.) Try to understand that you'll have to wait for this important information.
- Persevere. Even after you're eighteen, you're bound to

run into obstacles during your search. Contact an adoptees' rights advocacy group, learn what your rights are, and fight for them.

- Stay hopeful. Any piece of information can be the gateway to a genealogical breakthrough. This is true for anyone searching their roots, but especially for the adopted, who have a harder time finding information.
- Say "thank you." Among all the people who make your search more difficult, there will certainly be some who are glad to help you. Make sure these people know how much you appreciate their kind assistance.
- We're all in this together. Most people who know that they were adopted are curious about their past and their families. There are societies and books available to help you. The Yellow Pages list adoption support groups and service agencies, and other resources are listed at the end of this chapter.

People who are out of touch with one or both biological parents may certainly face difficulties in tracing their roots. Nevertheless, with understanding, patience, persistence, and optimism, they too can become adventurers in the mysterious and surprising world of genealogy.

Resources

REGISTERS/SUPPORT GROUPS/ADVOCACY FOR ADOPTEES

Adopted and Searching/Adoptee-Birthparent Reunion Registry
401 East 74th Street
New York, NY 10021
212-988-0110

Adoptee's Liberty Movement Association (ALMA)
850 Seventh Avenue
New York, NY 10019

> The foremost group in activism for adoptees' rights to information, they have set up one of the first Reunion Registries, which can be reached at 212-581-1568.

Adoptees and Birthparents in Search
P.O. Box 5551
West Columbia, SC 29171
803-796-4508

Adoptees' Search Right Association
Xenia, OH 45385
419-855-8439

Adoptees Together
Routel 1, Box 30-B-5
Climax, NC 27233

Adoptive Families of America
3333 Highway 100 North
Minneapolis, MN 55422
800-372-3300 (24-hour hotline)

American Adoption Congress
1000 Connecticut Avenue NW
Washington, DC 20036

Concerned United Birth Parents
200 Walker Street
Des Moines, IA 50317

The International Soundex Reunion Registry
P.O. Box 2312
Carson City, NV 89702

National Adoption Information Clearinghouse
11426 Rockville Pike, Suite 410
Rockville, MD 20852

ADOPTION AND OTHER FAMILY ISSUES

Askin, Jayne, with Molly Davis. *Search:*
A Handbook for Adoptees and Birthparents, **2d ed.**
Phoenix, AZ: Oryx Press, 1992.

> Every year adoption rights groups make more progress in establishing registers to connect adult adoptees with their biological parents. Askin offers a thorough guide to registers and searching aids in the United States.

Cohen, Shari. *Coping with Being Adopted.* **New York: Rosen Publishing Group, 1988.**

> A general guide for teenagers who may feel stress in their family and social life because they do not live with their biological parents. Includes a chapter on the pros and cons of searching for your birth parents.

Delany, Sarah Louise; Delany, Annie Elizabeth; and Hearth, Amy Hill. *Having Our Say: The Delany Sisters' First 100 Years.* **New York: Kodansha International, 1993.**

> Recently turned into a successful Broadway play, this is the blood-stirring memoir of two African American sisters

who saw both World Wars and the Depression and faced discrimination wherever they went, but their spirits wouldn't bend.

Engram, Eleanor. *Science, Myth, Reality: The Black Family in One-Half Century of Research.* **Westport, CT: Greenwood Press, 1982.**

Since the Great Depression, many factors have affected African Americans and their concept of family. New educational opportunities and other strides forward in civil rights have been tempered by an increased disillusionment among young blacks about the realities of their future, leading to crime, drug use, and a strain on the family unit.

Gormley, Myra Vanderpool. *Family Diseases: Are You at Risk?* **Baltimore: Genealogical Publishing, 1989.**

A book written specifically for family historians.

June, Lee N., ed. *The Black Family: Past, Present and Future: Perspectives of Sixteen Black Christian Leaders.* **Grand Rapids: Zondervan Publishing House, 1991.**

These are essays by theologians and ministers from several Christian denominations.

Lifton, Betty Jean. *Lost and Found: The Adoption Experience.* **New York: Perennial Library, 1988.**

The author was adopted and was curious about her own roots. When she became an adult she commenced a search for her heritage. This is the story of the trials and joys she faced as she slowly pieced together her family tree.

People Searching News

A periodical for adoptees/birth parents, published by J. E. Carlson & Associates, P.O. Box 22611, Ft. Lauderdale, FL 33335. Phone 305-370-7100.

Social Security
Office of Central Records Operations
Baltimore, MD 21201

Request form SSA-L997 to find a living relative by ordering his or her social security application. Not all requests will be honored (because this material is classified, they have the right to decide whether the request is warranted).

Social Security Administration Death Master File

This record of recently deceased Americans is available in microform from LDS Family History Centers. Check with your nearest branch. Includes millions of surnames, along with death place and date and place of burial.

Stevenson, Rosemary. *Index to Afro-American Reference Resources*. Westport, CT: Greenwood, 1990.

You can look up a wide range of subjects—education, health, insurance, housing, and many others—and this index will lead you to books, articles, pamphlets, and organizations that can answer your questions.

Wagonseller, Bill R.; Ruegamer, L. C.; and Harrington, M. C. *Coping in a Single-Parent Home*. New York: Rosen Publishing Group, 1992.

Learn to view your single-parent upbringing as a whole alternative family, rather than a traditional family missing a piece. This book focuses on teenagers; it offers advice on dealing with divorce and separation of the parents, and the teen's feelings of abandonment and guilt. Includes discussion on seeking the missing parent.

Chapter 9
Preserving Your Family History

More than once during your research you probably slammed down your pencil in frustration. If only your ancestors had jotted down what they knew about themselves and their families! They could easily have filled in the information you've spent months trying to get.

There are plenty of ways to organize and present your research, letting others know what you've accomplished and saving future genealogists in your family a good deal of work. And don't forget that you have the power to prevent a lot of frustration for the curious family historian of the twenty-second century. You can document *yourself*.

Consider starting a journal, and writing in it as often as you can. Keep copies of letters you write, or at least save those you receive. Old report cards, concert programs, and programs from school plays you were in also make good keepsakes. Even if you never write memoirs or an autobiography, it's still important to preserve the things that could be used to learn and write about you. In a hundred years, your great-grandchildren may be able to touch things that belong to you, to read your letters and journal.

Family Tree

The most basic way to present the genealogical research you have done is by filling in a family tree. A family tree can be a simple chart on a single sheet of paper. It can also be a work of art so splendid you'll want to have it framed.

The trunk of the tree represents the earliest known ancestral pair on a line of descent. Their children are shown as branches, their children as smaller branches, and so on.

Each entry on the tree should include the person's name,

date, and place of birth; date of marriage; date of death; and place of burial. You can leave blank spaces for missing information and fill it in if and when you get it. Sometimes an entire person is missing from the tree—say the unknown spouse of some remote ancestor. It's all right to leave a blank space for the missing person. Make a separate tree for each family line you research.

Although you're fussing over a lot of notes, your creativity can have free rein when you design the tree. If you or a friend or sibling can draw, feel free to make the family look like a real tree.

Oral History

Writing down stories and history was not an option for most of your African ancestors. Folks learned about their family's past by listening to stories retold by older clansmen and clanswomen. They learned the history of their people from the tales of the elder members of the village or town. The collection of all the tales makes up the people's oral history. In some societies, the Mandingo for example, there were professional storytellers called *griots*, who traveled from village to village, attracting crowds who eagerly listened to their tales.

Even if you don't want to be the *griot*, you can still be the caretaker of your family's oral history. You've already started by interviewing your relatives when you began your search.

Each tape you made contains the priceless personal memories of someone in your family. All the anecdotes and legends told by your various relatives make up your family history. Your tapes are the record. Collecting oral history is different from other parts of genealogical research, because you don't have to check other sources to prove the stories true. Usually you can't find proof, and often enough they're not *completely* true. No matter how "true" the story is, though, it's still entertaining, and it still contains real characteristics of your ancestors.

With a tape recorder (or if you're lucky, a video camera), you can create a timeless family treasure. Not just the words, but slang terms, tone of voice, gestures, and facial expressions can be part of this record.

Written History

A written family history is yet another way of preserving for the future what you've learned about your family. It can be anything from a short series of anecdotes or biographies about a handful of relatives to a 1,000-page masterwork like Alex Haley's *Roots*.

A family history is a book in which all the information from a genealogical research project is presented as a story. The writer adds historical background information about jobs, reasons for moves, and so forth, to basic information like names and dates. The family's oral history can also be woven into the narrative.

If the idea of writing an all-out family history seems like too much, relax. It's advisable to start with something smaller. You could write down some of the family anecdotes that you heard or recorded when you interviewed your relatives. Using your research as a guide, you could write a paragraph about everyone on your family tree. Then use these paragraphs to write a page about each family group you've researched. By doing this, you're taking the back door into writing a family history, because you can then use these paragraphs and pages to write something longer.

You might try writing a short biography about your favorite relative. If you can, write about his personality, using what you've learned from his letters, diaries, and family stories about him. Or pick an event in your family's history and build a short story around it.

No matter what you're thinking of writing, it can't hurt to have a look at Alex Haley's *Roots*. It is a remarkable mixture of fact and fiction from the pen of a professional writer. *Roots* begins with the birth of the author's last African-born ancestor (later enslaved in Virginia), and ends with the author's genealogical search for that very same ancestor. It's best to read the whole book, but if the length overwhelms you, choose sections that are of interest to you. Read about

Perhaps you will find that your research sparks an interest in visiting Africa. In the 1960s, the growing pride in African heritage produced a brief "Back to Africa" movement, as advertised in front of this Harlem bookstore in 1964.

West Africa, plantation life, Reconstruction, or the author's search itself in modern times. By his example, Haley provides help with the writing process, as well as inspiration, to the family historian. There is much to be learned from him, whether or not your ancestry is African.

Illustrations make fine "finishing touches" for a written story, biography, or family history. One illustration that should always be included is your family tree. It serves as a road map for the reader, making it easier to keep track of names and places in your story. In addition, photographs of relatives help make those people come alive as much as any description can. Photos of possessions of family members, such as dolls and other heirlooms, make great illustrations. If you ever visit the areas where your ancestors lived and worked, take your camera along for some original landscapes and cityscapes. If you're artistic, you can use an encyclopedia photo as a guide for an appropriate drawing; for example, a scene from a battle in which a relative took part.

If you want to be the heroine or hero to your great-great-grandchildren, you can leave behind more than a pile of research notes. Your detailed family tree or family history can be the pride of your family and save future genealogists lots of work.

When Africans were enslaved in the New World, they were generally forbidden to keep their names and retain their culture. Nevertheless, they knew who they were and where they had come from. Learning who *you* are and preserving your heritage with pride is one of the most important contributions you can make to African American culture.

Resources

WRITING YOUR FAMILY HISTORY

Bove, Tony. *The Art of Desktop Publishing.* **New York: Bantam Books, 1990.**

> How is a desktop program different from a word processor? Learn to make professional-looking documents with this introduction to the concepts of desktop.

Busch, David D. *The Complete Scanner Handbook for Desktop Publishing.* **Homewood, IL: Dow Jones-Irwin, 1990.**

> If you have access to the equipment, you can scan photos and handwritten letters onto your family history.

Cheney, Theodore A. Rees. *Writing Creative Nonfiction: How to Use Fiction Techniques to Make Your Nonfiction More Interesting, Dramatic and Vivid.* **Cincinnati, OH: Writer's Digest Books, 1987.**

> Make your family history more than just a list of dates and events. Keep it accurate, but make it read like a novel by using the tricks of the trade introduced in this guide.

The Chicago Manual of Style: The Essential Guide for Writers, Editors, and Publishers, **14th ed. Chicago: University of Chicago Press, 1993.**

> Easy to use, this manual has a great index. Its word is considered law by most publishing companies in the United States.

Fletcher, William P. *Record Your Family History.* **Berkeley, CA: Ten Speed Press, 1989.**

This is a guide to preserving your family's oral history on videotape and audiotape. It suggests interview techniques and sample questions, as well as giving examples of what to listen for in your relatives' stories.

McLaughlin, Paul. *A Family Remembers.* **North Vancouver, BC: Self-Counsel Press, 1993.**

This is an excellent, up-to-date guide on how to create a family memoir using video cameras and tape recorders.

Zinsser, William. *On Writing Well: An Informal Guide to Writing Nonfiction.* **New York: Harper & Row, 1985.**

A nonthreatening step-by-step manual for producing a clear piece of prose.

GREAT WRITING BY AFRICAN AMERICANS

Achebe, Chinua. *Things Fall Apart.* **New York: Astor-Honor, 1959.**

Achebe is one of the most celebrated of modern West African fiction writers. This is a tale of political discontent and personal struggle that communicates the African worldview to any reader.

Armah, Ayi Awei. *The Healers: An Historical Novel.* **London: Heinemann, 1979.**

The Asante people of West Africa are known for their profound connections with the spiritual and natural world, both on a personal level and through traditional seers. This novel takes that connection as the premise for a mesmerizing journey.

Cherrington, Clare. *Sunshine Island Moonshine Baby.* **London: Collins, 1984.**

A novel celebrating the Caribbean Islands' heritage. While recovering from a tonsillectomy, a girl named Sarah reluctantly attends her mother's sewing circle. She is enchanted, however, to hear stories about Caribbean life.

Daise, Ronald. *De Gullah Storybook.* **Beaufort, SC: G. O. G. Enterprises, 1989.**

> Gullah is the language and culture of the African Americans on the Georgia Sea Islands. These tales, some directly from Africa and some with roots in slavery and later, are told in both Gullah and English.

Egudu, Romanus N., and Nwoga, Donatus Ibe, eds. *Igbo Traditional Verse.* **London: Heinemann, 1973.**

> Read praise songs, war cries, prayers, curses, proverbs, and riddles in this collection of poetry in the oral tradition of the Igbo people of West Africa. Features the verse both in Igbo language and English.

Ellison, Ralph. *Invisible Man.* **New York: Random House, 1982.**

> This is *not* the novel on which the famous sci-fi movie was based. Rather it is a biting satire against racism by an African American, courageously published in 1932. It inspired countless other writers, filmmakers, and blacks in all walks of life.

Himes, Chester. *Works: The Collected Stories of Chester Himes.* **London: Allison & Busby, 1993.**

> This famous black author died in 1984 at the age of seventy-five. This is a collection of all his short fictions, including fictionalized essays about his own upbringing.

How Anansi Obtained the Sky God's Stories: An African Folktale from the Ashanti Tribe. **Chicago: Children's Press, 1991.**

> The famous trickster spider, Anansi, makes off with all the world's tales, jealously hoarded by the sky god Nyami. This retelling of the traditional Asante tale includes color illustrations and a cassette.

Hurston, Zora Neale. *Novels and Stories.* **New York: Library of America, 1995.**

This anthology includes the novels *Jonah's Gourd Vine, Their Eyes Were Watching God, Moses, Man of the Mountain,* and *Seraph on the Suwannee,* as well as selected stories. The works treat various aspects of African American life.

Johnson, Angela. *Toning the Sweep*. New York: Orchard Books, 1993.

On a visit to her grandmother Ola, who is dying of cancer in her house in the desert, fourteen-year-old Emmie hears many stories about the past and comes to a better understanding of relatives both dead and living.

Lotu, Denise. *Father and Son*. New York: Philomel Books, 1992.

This illustrated poetry-story for young people celebrates the relationship between an African American father and his son in the low country of South Carolina.

Medearis, Angela Shelf. *Picking Peas for a Penny*. Austin, TX: State House Press, 1990.

An illustrated book for young people, this is the story of an African family during the Great Depression. The tale is told from the point of view of a girl who helps to keep a farm functioning during those difficult years and learns the rewards of hard work.

Medina, Pablo. *The Marks of Birth*. New York: Farrar, Straus & Giroux, 1994.

An up-to-date novel about Caribbean immigrants to New York City. It describes their relationships with each other, their hopes and disappointments, and the racism and stereotyping they face.

Morrison, Toni. *Beloved*. New York: Knopf, 1987.

Besides being a good story, this novel is an interesting social and historical commentary. Morrison describes the urban life of working-class and educated African Americans in Cincinnati, Ohio.

————. *Tar Baby*. **New York: Knopf, 1981.**

Racial identity and the self-esteem of African Americans are explored in this novel, as well as blacks' relationships among themselves and with others, shaped by their self-image.

Glossary

abolitionism   Advocacy of the elimination of slavery.

bigotry   Intolerance to differences from one's own position, usually in race, religious, or political matters.

commodity   An article that is bought and sold.

denomination   A religious body made up of a number of local congregations having similar beliefs.

diaspora   The collective dispersion of a religious and/or ethnic group.

disenfranchised   To be deprived of rights.

distillery   A place where alcoholic liquors are purified.

docile   Easily managed.

emancipation   Liberation; term used to describe the release of blacks from slavery.

epitaph   An inscription in memory of a deceased person.

gazetteer   A geographical dictionary.

generation   A group of people who constitute a single step in the line of descent from an ancestor.

hearsay   Unconfirmed rumor.

humanitarian   One who promotes human welfare.

indentured servitude   The binding of workers by contract for a specific period of time.

integration   The end of segregation; the act of bringing disenfranchised groups into equal membership in society.

lynching   To put to death by mob action without due process of law.

manumission   Freedom from slavery.

mulatto   A person of mixed black and white ancestry.

pedigree   A record of a line of ancestors.

plantation   A large agricultural estate worked by resident laborers.

Reconstruction   The period of twelve years following the Civil War when efforts were made to remedy the social, physical, and economic destruction the war had caused in the South.

secede To withdraw formally.

segregation The act of separation or isolation.

solidarity A union of ideas or interests by a group.

squalor A state of filth or degradation.

suffrage The right to vote.

Thirteenth Amendment A constitutional amendment, ratified in 1865, abolishing slavery.

transcript A written, printed, or typed copy.

treatise A formal written account.

Index

A

Abolition, 35, 49–50, 117, 134
adoption, 149–151
adoption register, 152–153
Africa, 4–8, 25–28, 38–44, 59–60
Alabama, 1, 37, 51, 52, 56
American Anti-Slavery Society, 50
American Genealogical Lending Library (AGLL), 132, 147
ancestors, tracing, 91
archives, 99, 121–122, 132
Arkansas, 37, 51, 52, 56
Atlanta, Georgia, 57

B

Back to Africa, 4–6
Baltimore, Maryland, 56, 138
birth certificate, 96, 98, 122
Boston, Massachusetts, 31, 56, 138
Bureau of Refugees, Freedmen and Abandoned Lands, 52

C

Canada, 49, 60
Caribbean
  immigrants from, 58
  music, 59
  slaves in, 1, 6, 31, 35
census, federal, 116–125
Charleston, North

Carolina, 34
Charleston, South Carolina, 52
Chicago, Illinois, 56–57
Christianity, 30, 33, 134
Christian Recorder, 135
Church of Jesus Christ of Latter-day Saints, The, 132, 145
civil rights, 8
  movement, 3–4
Civil Rights Act of 1964, 3
Civil War, 35, 51, 133
"colored troops." *See* troops, "colored"
computer genealogy, 144–146
Confederate States of America, 51
congregation, integrated, 134
cotton gin, 37
culture, slaves cut off from, 8, 58

D

dance forms, African, 59
database management, 145–146
death certificate, 96, 122
deed book, county, 132–133, 138
Defender, Chicago, 56–57
desktop publishing, 144
Detroit, Michigan, 56
diaries, 94, 98, 131
diaspora, African cultural, 49–60
directory, town, 121
Dominican Republic, 58

Douglass, Frederick, 49, 123

E

Emancipation Proclamation, 51, 118, 120–121, 131
empires, African, 25
England, 27–28, 30, 35, 49, 58
estate records, 132
evidence, documented, 94–97

F

families, nontraditional, 149–151
family group sheets, 93–94
Family History Library, 132
family history, written, 158–160
family tree, 4, 156–157, 160
Florida, 51, 52, 56
France, 27, 35
Free African Society, 136
freedmen, 51–52, 133

G

Garnet, Henry Highland, 49–50
Garrison, William Lloyd, 50
Genealogical Data Communications (GEDCOM), 145
genealogical society, 100
Generations Library, 145
genetic disease, 149
Georgia, 35, 37, 51, 56

gifts, deeds of, 132
gravestone, rubbing, 98
griot, 157
Guinea, 27
"Guinea Town," 135
Gullah, 58–59

H
Haiti, 33, 58
Haley, Alex, 4–6, 158–160
heritage, celebrating, 1–8
Houston, Texas, 57

I
illiteracy, 6, 119
indentured servitude, 30
interlibrary loan, 100–101
International Genealogy Index (IGI), 132
Internet, 101, 144, 146, 148
interracial union, 122–125
interview
  self-, 91
  with relatives, 92–93

J
Jacksonville, Florida, 52
Jamestown, Virginia, 29

K
Kansas, 50, 53, 56
King, Martin Luther, Jr., 1–3
Kwanzaa, 9, 10

L
land ownership, 51–53
language, Gullah, 58–59
legends, family, 91–92
letters, 94, 131, 158
library, 99–101, 132
Library of Congress, 139
Lincoln, Abraham, 50–51

Lloyd's Register, 139
Louisiana, 37, 51, 52
L'Ouverture, Toussaint, 33
lynching, 37, 53

M
Malcolm X, 3
manumission, deeds of, 122, 131
marriage certificate, 96, 122
Maryland, 31
Middle Passage, 137
  horrors of, 27–28
migration, black, 53–58
Milwaukee, Wisconsin, 56
Mississippi, 37, 51, 52, 53, 56
Missouri, 52
mixed marriages. *See* interracial unions
Montgomery, Alabama, 3
Mormons. *See* Church of Jesus Christ of Latter-day Saints, The
mortgage deeds, 132
mulatto, 123–125
music, African, 59

N
name. *See* surname
National Archives, 133–134, 137, 139
Native Americans, 30, 123
Newport, Rhode Island, 31, 138
New York, New York, 56, 138
North Carolina, 31, 34, 51, 56
northern migration, 54–57

O
On-line Catalog of the Library of Congress (OCLC), 101
oral history, 8, 91, 157–158
organization of search, 93–94

P
Parks, Rosa, 3
pedigree charts, 93–94
Personal Ancestral File (PAF), 145
Philadelphia, Pennsylvania, 56, 138
photographs, 98, 160
ports, slave, 138–139
Powell, Colin, 1
prenuptial agreements, 132
Pritchard, "Gullah Jack," 34

Q
Quakers, 35, 134
questionnaire, family, 92

R
racism, 1, 3, 49
railroad workers, 136
rebellion, fear of, 6, 31–34, 37, 119
Reconstruction, 51–53, 62–65
records
  church, 134
  military, 96, 133–134
  railroad, 136
  ship, 6, 138–139
"Red Summer," 56
relatives
  interviewing, 92–93
  talking to, 91
religious leadership, 3, 33–34
Roanoke, Virginia, 138

Roots, 4, 158–160
Roots (software), 145
roots, African, 1, 4, 6,
    8, 59

S
St. Louis, Missouri, 56
sale, bill of, 133, 138
Salem, Massachusetts,
    31
Savannah, Georgia, 138
segregation, 4, 56
sharecropping, 53
Sherman, William T.,
    52
Singleton, Benjamin
    "Pap," 53–54
slave codes, 33
slave owners, tracing,
    100, 131–133
slavery, 1, 4
    in African societies,
    25
    life in, 30–34
slaves
    illegal trade in, 37
    importation banned, 35

slave trade
    modern, 25–30
    end of, 35–37
slave traders, 4, 6, 27
Soundex code, 116–117
South America
    slaves in, 6, 27, 35
    music from, 59
South Carolina, 31, 35,
    51, 52, 56
surname, 4, 58, 94, 99–
    100, 146
    adopting new, 117–
    121
    African, 4, 6, 100
    missing in census, 117
    tracing, 91, 94, 116–
    117

T
Tafel Matching System,
    146
tape-recording, 93, 157
tax returns, 96–97
Tennessee, 37, 51, 56
Texas, 37, 51
tradition, oral, 8, 94, 120

troops, colored, 133–134
Truth, Sojourner, 49
Tubman, Harriet, 49
Turner, Nat, 34

U
Underground Railroad,
    49, 135

V
Vesey, Denmark, 34
Virginia, 34, 51, 53
vital statistics, 92, 94–
    96, 156–157
vote, right to, 52–53

W
Washington, DC, 56
western migration, 53–
    54
wills, 8, 96, 131–132
women's suffrage, 49
word processing, 144
World War I, 54–55
World War II, 57

ABOUT THE AUTHORS
Anne E. Johnson has done extensive research on the African roots of African American art forms. **Adam Merton Cooper** became interested in African linguistics and the cultural diaspora when he began to trace his own genealogy as a child. Both authors hold degrees from the University of Wisconsin.

ILLUSTRATION CREDITS
Cover, © Nancy Brown/The Image Bank; cover inset and pp. 2, 5, 7, 26, 28, 29, 32, 36, 50, 54, 55, 57, 60, 97, 118, 124, 135, 159, BETTMAN. *Color insert:* p. 2, Eliot Elisofon, National Museum of African Art, Eliot Elisofon Photographic Archives, Smithsonian Institution; p. 3, © J. J. Foxx/NYC; p. 4, © Fred Phillips/ Impact Visuals; p. 5, © Meryl Levin/Impact Visuals; p. 6, © Brian Palmer/ Impact Visuals; p. 7, © Harvey Finkle/Impact Visuals; p. 8, © Ken Martin/ Impact Visuals; p. 9, © Robert Fox/Impact Visuals; p. 10, © Judy Janda/Impact Visuals; p. 11, © Clark Jones/Impact Visuals; pp. 12, 13, © K. Condyles, Impact Visuals; p. 14, BETTMAN; p. 15, © Wm. Cochrane/Impact Visuals; p. 16, AP/ Wideworld Photos.

LAYOUT AND DESIGN
Kim Sonsky